THE ROAD HOME

THE

ROAD

HOME

ELIZA THOMAS

Algonquin Books

of Chapel Hill

1997

Published by
ALGONQUIN BOOKS OF CHAPEL HILL
Post Office Box 2225
Chapel Hill, North Carolina 27515-2225

a division of
Workman Publishing
708 Broadway
New York, New York 10003

Library of Congress Cataloging-in-Publication Data
Thomas, Eliza.
      The road home / by Eliza Thomas.
         p.   cm.
      ISBN 1-56512-169-4
      1. Thomas, Eliza.   2. Vermont—Biography.   3. Vermont
—Social life and customs.   4. Country life—Vermont.
      I. Title.
CT275.T545A3   1997
974.3'009734—dc21   96-53975
      [B]   CIP

10   9   8   7   6   5   4   3   2   1
First Edition

For my family, with much love

CONTENTS

ACKNOWLEDGMENTS

THANKS TO JULIAN and Amelia for their enormous part in this. Thanks to Liz Darhansoff, my agent, for shepherding and guiding this book along the road. Thanks to Elisabeth Scharlatt, my editor, for giving it a wonderful home. Thanks to Julie Marden, friend and writers' group, for her encouragement and clear perspective. And thanks to my sister Abby, who urged me to write this book in the first place, for her insights that illuminated the way, for her generosity, for her hope at the beginning and throughout.

PROLOGUE: HUMMINGBIRDS

I ONCE HELD a hummingbird in my hand. I was on my lunch hour, walking around downtown Boston, and saw it lying on the sidewalk right in front of a bank window. I picked it up because I was afraid people would step on it. It was still alive, breathing as fast and as imperceptibly as you might imagine a hummingbird would breathe, but otherwise limp and motionless. I ran back to my office, holding my own breath the whole way, holding in my hand this amazing thing, a creature the size of an almond, weightless, fragile, all shimmer and no substance, only there it was, lying in the palm of my hand. I could stroke its feathers, feel the prick of its long beak. I worked for a small, busy immigrants' rights organization. When I got to the office, I telephoned the Audubon Society for advice. "I have a stunned hummingbird," I started to say, when the hummingbird flew out of my hand.

It took hours to free it from the office. We had to turn out all the lights and tape newspapers to the windowpanes so that the only light it would see would be the actual open part of the window. Work, at least my work, came to a standstill. The hummingbird was probably terrified; I know I was. All that mattered to me at that moment was giving this bird its freedom. But the story ended well: at some point it simply swooped out the window and headed toward the Boston Common.

A few years later, I moved to Vermont. It was magic, I thought, when one day I saw a hummingbird there. I had no idea that hummingbirds came so far north, and it seemed a special sign to see this exotic friend who might have been the very same bird I rescued and then rescued from being rescued.

It was also rewarding to see it, as I was beginning to feel very disappointed in wildlife. My neighbors right down the same road spoke casually about the wild turkeys that gathered in their field, the herons and pileated woodpeckers, the families of baby foxes, the many deer with fawns, even the solitary baby moose, strolling down the road one day. From my equally rural cabin, however, I saw nothing. I know there was a skunk, because it sprayed my dog twice. There were raccoons that got into the garbage. There were mice; oh, were there mice. There were deer that ate up the garden and the lilac bushes, but they came only at night and I never saw them. Then one day there was that one hummingbird, suddenly appearing out of nowhere, hovering at the apple blossoms, flitting across the field, perching at the top of the birch tree, favoring us especially.

Or so I wanted to feel. To make sure my hummingbird would stick around, I bought a hummingbird feeder. The stores seemed suddenly full of hummingbird feeders, and my friend Julian agreed that it seemed the thing to do. At the time it was the only plastic thing we had, at least in the yard. It was, and still is, a red plastic dome set in a round tray. The base has little yellow plastic flowers glued to it. The center of each of these little flowers is a little hole, and that is what the hummingbirds suck the man-made nectar out of. So now, instead of flitting and swooping through the apple blossoms, appearing from nowhere, hanging in the air amid the bee balm and lilies and roses and sweet william that we've planted, they generally head straight for the red plastic dome full of one part sugar to three parts water. It definitely works—we definitely have resident hummingbirds year after year now—but I feel sort of terrible about it (though not nearly as terrible as I do about the mouse poison that I put out). It seems unhealthy, addictive, like TV: no vitamins, no culture, no redeeming qualities. "You'll rot your beak with all that sugar water," I overheard Julian mutter one day, batting away at a couple of hummingbirds as he opened the screen door.

The feeder hangs outside the narrow porch, on a long, thin wire. Julian had the idea of spraying the wire with insect repellent in order to discourage the ants, but they are never discouraged for long. So there hangs the hummingbird feeder, the air around it positively thrumming with hummingbird life, and there, also, flows the never-ending stream of ants, making their way single file down the long, thin, repellently sprayed wire, on their own narrow beeline to the plastic daisy holes. In they go, and in most of them stay. After a while, it becomes clear that the hummingbird feeder is full of dead ants. The only way to clean them out is to force water into the top of the feeder, so that the ant corpses come flying out through the little flower holes. This is a chore that we both put off as long as possible.

There is another problem, or not exactly a problem, since I certainly shouldn't so glibly describe my young daughter as a problem. But she is here, and since her arrival we have acquired, one way or another, a lot more bright plastic objects. I sit on my narrow porch in rural Vermont on this Indian summer afternoon and see, apart

from the old apple orchard and the now-faded hummingbird feeder, one plastic yellow-and-turquoise slide; one
yellow-and-green scooter; one yellow truck with a red
steering wheel; one green-and-white polka-dot wading
pool, with matching beach ball and donut tube; one plastic clothesline with various brightly colored plastic clothespins; two headless yellow duckies (my dog bites the heads
off); and three stray plastic beads. Hummingbirds zoom
about everywhere, hopelessly confused by the bright colors, hovering pathetically over the steering wheel of the
truck, perching on the clothesline to peer intently at the
clothespins. One of them—in my new casual familiarity
with wildlife I like to call him the Juvenile, because he
seems somehow less knowledgeable, less sure of himself (I
am also quite certain it is a male), and not quite as sleek as
the adult hummingbirds—even poked a small hole in the
beach ball.

I don't know how to sort this all out, how, or whether,
to try to explain to the hummingbirds not to be attracted
to bright plastic objects unless they contain sugar water. I
can't think how to extricate the ants from the whole complicated relationship, either. Hummingbirds are still magic
to me, and I hate to see them make silly fools of themselves, acting like such birdbrains over plastic clothespins. I

don't want any more plastic things myself, either. But then the other day my next-door neighbor, surreptitiously on her way to the dump before her family could protest, offered me another yellow truck. It was one that her children had really loved when they were toddlers. It was the kind that I knew my daughter coveted. Now that she has it, she is full of pride, and she glows with happiness when she climbs into the driver's seat. How could I say no?

THE CABIN

AN INTRODUCTION: BEFORE AND AFTER

IF I'D HAD the foresight to look ahead years ago, I would not have imagined that life would be turning out the way it is. If I had been so clear-minded, it would have all been different, anyway. In any case, I'm sure I could not have seen myself at age forty-eight, living in an old Boy Scout cabin in the middle of New England, perennially looking for work to support myself, my old dog, and my very young daughter. However did you land there? I would have asked, a little worriedly. But I might have been a bit in awe as well. I came of age in the sixties and was easily impressed by alternative lifestyles, although I had little grasp of the basics.

BEFORE MOVING TO my cabin, I lived in Boston for many years. Decades, actually. Except for a few brief forays, I had stayed on indefinitely after college, although I always considered myself in transit, in a period of transition, before life really began. This gave me lots of leeway, I thought.

Anyway, I had always thought home was the memory of someplace you grew up in; I never considered that it might be someplace you made. My family had moved around often when I was a child, living somewhere different every two years or so. I wasn't sure exactly where to say I'd come from if anyone asked; it could have been any number of places. A chance and random sensation—a cool breeze on my bare arm, for example, or a certain reflection of light, or some fragment of music I'd learned long ago—and I'd be taken back in time; I'd imagine shafts of sun through a tumble of clouds, fingers of heaven illuminating one special, lucky spot: home. It was always in the permanent past. Everywhere else was temporary.

I'm not sure what I was waiting for, but I was over forty when I came to my senses, at least to some degree. Temporarily or not, I'd lived in the Boston area for more than half my life. All that leeway had led nowhere; all I had to show for those years was a long series of false starts. Time had been running out, and I hadn't been paying attention.

I DIDN'T YET know how to piece together a new life; I just knew that I badly needed a change, and the cabin in Vermont that I'd bought a few years before seemed a possible starting point. It was there, available, affordable, far away but not too far; my dog, Lily, liked it, it was pretty, and it was mine.

It was also tiny and somewhat drafty and had some serious structural inadequacies. Unexpected problems arose with the passing seasons and the accompanying cold, wet, snowy, muddy, and dry spells. In time, my friend Julian started coming up on the weekends from Cambridge, and we threw ourselves into the many projects that presented themselves. Working on the place took on an interest and a passion of its own. We cleared land, planted gardens, dreamed about running water, and fantasized about a new septic system. We learned how to build, and the house grew bigger, although more and more strangely shaped with each addition.

Our friendship changed shape, too, along with the house, finally entering the realm of coupledom. Possibilities grew; we could make room for a child. And major changes occurred: I signed on to an adoption program, and after much agonizing and many delays I finally brought Amelia home.

For me, preparing for life with a child has centered around my cabin and the four acres it sits on. It really is home for now, with memories already made and memories in the making; but as it has turned out, making it home has had as much to do with the preparation as with the place itself. And that process, somewhat late in life, often haphazard, always ongoing, is what this book is about.

As I write this, Amelia is here, ever present. She runs from room to room, dropping toys and clothes and pots and pans in her wake, leaving behind surprise bags of miscellany. So she is here in this book as well from the very beginning, turning up at odd moments, at one age or another. She insists on this, and she is probably right.

SOMEPLACE JUST RIGHT

I BOUGHT THE cabin eight years ago. I had some money that my aunt had left me, and it was making me very anxious and guilty; I worried that I would fritter it away. So I decided to buy some land with it, a little house maybe. It would be a wise and wonderful thing to do. One long, late summer that stretched into fall, I set out to find one within my means and drove with Lily all through northern New England.

It was our quest, and our recreation too. Every weekend I would pick at random a region of one state or another, and off we'd go. I became uncharacteristically brazen about stopping into real estate offices in small towns, where Lily and I would pile into the salesperson's car to be driven to whatever property was cheap enough to consider. It was a little like hitchhiking in the good old days, only without the terrible fears and anxiety.

It was also interesting. I would start each drive knowing nothing, and at the end I would have learned something I'd never expected. I'd know that the salesman used to be a bank executive but had burned out and moved his entire family to this tiny town, all the way from New Jersey. Or that the saleswoman had taken up real estate that very same year. She hoped to make a bundle but, more important, also hoped to have enough free time to get to know her teenage son, from whom she felt estranged and with whom she had just started skydiving lessons. Another admitted that he liked getting to know people, but not very intimately or for very long, and that was why this job was perfect for him: we'd all get out of his car at the end of the day. I learned that it cost a small fortune to bring electricity to anywhere off the path not already beaten by electric companies. I learned that the words "cozy" and "quaint" in real estate ads really meant "claustrophobic" and "dilapidated." If the ad didn't mention where the house was, it generally meant that the house was two feet from a main road. "Convenient location" meant basically *in* the main road.

I learned a lot about my own taste and needs. I liked trees, but at a distance. I liked the smell of manure and the look of cows. I found that views of small white villages with church steeples gave me deep and anxious melancholy, especially in the fall, like some distant, ancient, very sad memory; but whose memory, or of what, I could not say. Houses in the woods reminded me, also unhappily, of Robert Frost poems. On the other hand, I loved the shape of the land, the mounds of hills, the open pastures and narrow valleys. I loved the summer smells and the green everything and everywhere of the New England countryside, so much beauty and life piling into such a short growing season. I did not let myself consider the New England winter. I learned that I wanted power and water and most definitely a phone line, privacy but not seclusion. Beyond those requirements, I didn't know what I was looking for. Someplace to live? Someplace to camp? Someplace to build? I had no real idea.

The first property we saw was a cozy and quaint three-room cabin in a remote area of the Northeast Kingdom. It was on a dirt road, and it listed dramatically to one side. It was homebuilt, the rooms were tiny and dark, and the ceiling was unnaturally low, as if they had run out of wood when they were building it. Near an up-and-coming ski resort, the location alone was worth the price, or so the real estate salesman, who wrote poetry in his spare time, said without much conviction.

The second property was a two-room structure nestled

in a huge cloud of mosquitoes near an established resort lake, owned by a very young couple who were obviously frantic to sell it. There was a toilet sitting in the front lawn, which I asked about. "Ah," they said. We all stood around for a while, swatting away at mosquitoes, awkward and polite. I could hear the speedboats right from the front door.

We saw a homemade log cabin powered by six car batteries all in a row in the middle of the woods. "Entering God's Country," warned a sign on the road. We saw a mobile home on five beautiful acres near nothing in particular. It was squat and green and undeniably ugly, but it had a certain charm as well as a beautiful old white clapboard shed. Taking that as a cue, I sought other old clapboard structures, was shown a wonderful schoolhouse at the end of a dirt road (too expensive) and an old post office right on a main road, with a mail slot from the living room right to the bathroom (also too expensive). We went on a spree of seeing anything and everything: hunting camps way too far in the woods; strange, lopsided houses whose inner core would reveal a battered old trailer; old capes whose floors and roofs had rotted completely through; hilltop huts with spectacular views and nothing else; and one inaccessible plot of once-cleared land with a big pile of old timber—the original barn.

I was lucky: by the fall I wound up with someplace just right, a one-room cabin on four acres in a small valley. The cabin was little and set up on cinder blocks; it was a place to live in or camp at or build or rebuild, so I didn't have to decide right away which it would be. It was on a good dirt road not too far from the highway, and it even had a small willow tree. The four acres were an overgrown hillside of unkempt old apple trees, edged by a hemlock grove and a line of maple trees on one side and a hemlock forest on the other. It had power and water and a phone line and it was as nice as anything I could afford. It seemed like now or never, and so I bought it, using up most of my money. And that is why I'm here.

Because it is in a small valley and because the boundary is all trees, when I stand on my porch in the full leaves of summer I can truthfully say, "Everything I see belongs to me." I do not have long views, see no sad steeples. When I first started coming on weekends, I would walk around in wonder as I fell in love with the place. Sometimes I'd actually lie on the ground facedown and hug it; I loved that it was mine. Someday all this will be yours, I'd tell Lily. Now, years later, I say the same to Amelia, saving Lily her favorite place under the nearest apple tree.

• • •

HERE COMES AMELIA now. She is just two years old, and very proud of herself. She has reached the stage of having many strong and conflicting opinions. She is vehement, if unintelligible, about what she wants to eat, what she wants to eat it in, where she wants to sit, where she wants me to sit, and what she wants to wear. Lately, it is string cheese and grapes in a blue cup on the porch, dressed in polka dots. I sit on the porch with her, and Lily gets some string cheese, too.

My daughter has straight, flyaway hair that she hates to have washed. Sometimes it's quite sticky. When she smiles, it is with all her heart and soul. She is rather slight but has caught up to well within the curve on the growth chart my pediatrician gave me as a reference. Her day care teachers recently had individual conferences with the parents, providing a personalized chart for each child. Amelia's included "great sense of humor" and "loves scarves."

THE CABIN

AS FAR AS I know, the cabin we live in was originally a Boy Scout cabin, thirteen feet wide, thirty-two feet long. The first owner moved it to this piece of land twenty-five years ago from a Boy Scout troop campground in New Hampshire. He had sawed it in half somehow and brought it in two trips on a flatbed trailer truck. And so it became a hunting camp for a while, providing shelter from the wind and rain but little else. Sometime later, an out-of-state "flatlander" passing down this dirt road one day fell in love with the place, and on impulse he made an offer and bought it. Handy as a carpenter, he insulated it all around, then lined the entire inside with rough wood paneling. He built cabinets for a kitchen area, shelves for the bathroom corner, and two rows of bunk beds down half of one wall. A spring well was dug up the hill, and something of a septic system installed. He covered up the dingy shiplap siding with rustic board-and-batten, screened in the narrow front porch, framed in a small skylight, reshingled the roof, and put in a shiny new stovepipe chimney for a woodstove. With running water, toilet, shower, electric power, and phone, voilà! It was a luxurious weekend getaway for family and friends.

Eventually it again changed hands, bought by more flatlanders, a young couple who moved up and lived for a year in this one-room cabin with their newborn daughter. They added their own touches of home: wall-to-wall carpet for the living and sleeping area, linoleum for the kitchen, a new refrigerator, a propane heater to replace the authentic but unreliable woodstove, an improved water heater for the corner bathroom. They stuffed insulation around the cabin's base and undersides, strengthened its footings, devised various systems to keep the pipes from freezing, expanded the septic system. Then they started to build a much bigger house down the road.

Thus, by the time that I, yet another flatlander, bought it, the structure was something more than a camp, something less than a house. It seemed perfect both for what it was and for what it was not, although now, after eight years, it looks quite different. My first and second additions, off its back, provide living and sleeping space, so I've gradually expanded the kitchen to fill most of the original cabin. I've added army-grade counters and cabinets I found at a building salvage store. I've dismantled the bunk beds and set two of them upright to stand as ready-made walls for a closet; the other two are somewhere in the shed. At some point, I put down yet another floor.

A Boy Scout cabin is not at all what I dreamed of owning, but it has its appeal. The rough wood paneling provides a kind of rosy glow in the cabin, and people look especially good in its warm colors. Stubborn blemishes and the harsher signs of age are all softened somewhat, or so I like to think when I look in the bathroom mirror. Maybe this is just another way of saying that it is rather dark inside, which it is, but I still see a benevolence in its soft shadows. It has nice acoustics, too, dampened gently by the wooden walls and the low ceiling. It feels quite safe and comfortable inside.

Overall, however, it is not strikingly beautiful, or interestingly old, or very convenient. With each passing year its drawbacks accumulate; it gets draftier and leakier all the time and the floor bounces and shakes even with Amelia's light step. After all its transformations, its dimensions are still more suitable for a small child than for the average adult: the walls are a scant five feet high, the roof rises to a shallow peak, and the windows are small and so low that most people have to sit down in order look through them.

Maybe this is part of its charm, though; it retains some spirit and memory of childhood adventures, and represents not quite the real world. This may be why all its owners have gone to such great lengths with it. Or maybe, with its small windows and rather claustrophobic ceilings, it is a little like a boat: the urge is strong to paint it and caulk it, shore up its sides, secure its moorings, bail it out, keep it afloat. So that is what I've done, with a lot of help from Julian.

AND HERE IS Julian, a formal introduction. He and I were introduced to each other in Cambridge by our dogs. It was a companionable way to start off; there was a whole community of dog walkers at the park we went to. We all knew one another by our dogs; Julian was "Spot's owner." Spot was a Lab mix, black with a single smudge of white on her chest, hence her name. Julian called her "Spotty," which I thought was sort of sweet. He looked very nice, and so did she; clearly, he loved her, treated her with the deference and respect she deserved. She was rather matronly, dignified and a bit fat, but she had a long, slender nose and long, delicate legs like a deer. She'd prance when she felt particularly gay, suddenly light on her feet; it was wonderful to see. My dog, Lily, is black with a smudge of white on her chest, too, short and square and well grounded, but back then she could run almost as fast as Spot. They made an odd couple, Mutt and Jeff, and they were always glad to see each other. And so were we. He was a plumber trained in biology. I was a clerical assistant with a background in music. We all started to take our walks together.

Over the years, our friendship's center of gravity gradually shifted northward to my cabin in Vermont. After I moved up full-time, Julian began to visit regularly; I know the place already reminded him of home. We worked side by side on the cabin and additions and cleared out space to plant our gardens; at some point we acknowledged that we were building a future together. Spot found her own place in the kitchen in front of the heater—of course we called it Spot's spot—and she was the one to discover the frog pond in the neighboring field. I am sure that Lily looked forward to their visits, and so did I.

Now, some years and several additions later, we still do.

CLEARING

OF COURSE, THE place isn't perfect. Its major drawback as I see it, and Julian agrees, is that it is in a little valley, rather than on top of a high hill. The sun sets early over the hill, and earlier still over the many hemlock trees on the hill. Hemlock and maple trees hem us in and threaten to take over the whole old orchard. Clearing the land was the first major project, and it took several years to begin to make headway.

The first year, I bought a scythe. I had images of myself out on the hillside in the long autumn afternoon sun, swinging my scythe with graceful, fluid movements, long grass falling softly, silently, or with maybe just a light swishing sound. The men in the tool store seemed surprised but politely helpful when I chose my scythe from where it was hanging very high on the wall (at eye level were power tools, which I did not consider). When I described the underbrush on my land, they chose a blade that was quite a bit wider and shorter than the one I'd had in my mind, explaining that I needed a good, stiff edge to clear the brush. "This blade would clear young trees as thick as this," the older of them said, holding up his strong, calloused little finger. He demonstrated how to cut and yank, cut and yank. He approved of my fall schedule. He said that in the old days, that was how the road crews worked, adding that now, of course, they used brush hogs.

I didn't dare ask what those were. And so, with odd images of past and present, I brought my prize back to the cabin. Practice as I might, however, I could not get anywhere with my scythe. It was so terribly heavy. I wrestled with trees as thick and as thin as any finger on my hand, in vain I swished away at wide patches of long grass, and it wasn't long before I was totally humiliated by my scythe.

After some thought, I went to a different store to spare myself embarrassment. There, I bought a small saw, and with that I sawed down an entire hemlock grove of at least fifty small trees. It took only one weekend of solid sawing, but I clenched the saw so tightly that my finger joints almost froze shut permanently. Julian, meanwhile, had unearthed a machete I had brought back from South America in a brief previous life as a hippie world traveler.

He did quite well with it when he visited one weekend, hacking away enthusiastically through the hillside to liberate the apple trees. I tried the next weekend, but I was easily discouraged; I must have left it under a pile of vegetation near the frog pond because the machete vanished forever. I suppose I should have missed it—I'd brought the thing all the way back from Colombia, through all sorts of customs posts—but I really didn't mind losing it. I now had my sights set on power tools.

Eventually, I bought the top of the line in weedwhackers. I reasoned that it was my vacation pay. Instead of lolling around, I would destroy vegetation. It was very expensive, very noisy, very powerful. One swing of this mean machine was worth a million swings of the scythe, by then hanging high on a hook in the shed. I was the Path of Destruction. Young trees and underbrush didn't have a chance, and gradually the shape of the hillside and the old semiwild orchard began to emerge from beneath.

The final blow we struck for civilized landscaping was with Julian's chain saw. I think he'd always wanted one, and after I moved up here he found the perfect excuse. He held that hemlock trees absorbed light and that our garden would not thrive in their presence. One night, after several beers on our narrow porch, he further postulated that black holes were in fact small planets covered with hemlock forests. Light never escapes such an environment, he argued. We were in danger of being sucked into the void, where gravity compounds itself and everything is eternally dark. And so with his saw he planned to cut down all hemlocks within the changing path of the sun's seasons; his goal was to maximize sunlight on the cabin and its immediate vicinity. And so he tried to do. Anyway, he cut down some very big trees. It is still shadier than we would like, but it is a valley, after all. We can't hack down the whole hill.

Years later, however, the land remains still only partially cleared. Other things have taken priority, and it has resisted efforts at reform. We could hire a man with a brush hog, which turns out to be a very powerful mower on a long neck, but we haven't done so. Pesky little hemlock trees and fresh young maples still crop up everywhere; some of the oldest apple trees are slowly giving up the ghost. The best we can do is to maintain it as an overgrown old orchard on an older pasture that used to be even older forestland. It is quite interesting and beautiful the way it is though, being on the edge, in between.

WATER, PART ONE

BEING WAY OUT in the country, my cabin had its own water supply, the "spring" up on the hill, and a septic system, which we will not discuss. The water was "gravity fed," which meant that the source was so much higher than the house that the water simply flowed into the pipes and out the faucets, with no pump, no holding tank required. Since I had never, ever thought about the necessity of a holding tank and pump, the simplicity of this system made absolute sense to me. Nothing complicated, nothing I did not understand that might go awry, I thought innocently and somewhat incoherently.

Well, there were fundamental snags. The one that loomed first was the weather: it is cold in Vermont. The inside pipes froze on a nightly basis if it got cold enough, and the line from the well to the house froze on an annual basis, especially if there was no insulating blanket of snow.

I tried everything anybody suggested. To combat the problem of the interior pipes freezing, I bought yards and yards of heat tape, something I'd never heard of before, and coiled it around any pipe within reach. Julian came up with all kinds of insulating materials I'd also never heard of—Bubble Wrap, foils, foams, fiberglass, Styrofoam—and helped pack it around vulnerable spots.

The cabin was set up for weekend use, and the pipes could be drained of water before leaving the cabin un-heated in the cold and wind. The former owner carefully and patiently walked me through each step, and I had the instructions taped up to my refrigerator. I'd first turn off the valve that let the water in. Then I'd open up all the faucets, turn some valves behind the toilet, flush it to empty it of water, and pour some ecologically correct pink antifreeze into the bowl and tank. I'd turn off the water heater, located in the bathroom, and drain it too, through a hose I'd stick down the shower drain. I'd open the plug in what I learned were the traps, the curvy pipes under the bathroom and kitchen sinks, and let the trapped water gush into a pan. That was basically it, though I remember it being very much more complicated. I had little under-standing of what I was doing, beyond following the direc-tions to the letter. I'd carry the worn instruction sheet around with me as I turned each valve on or off, opened or closed each faucet, muttering "Lefty, loosy, righty, tighty," just as the former owner had suggested when he saw my ignorant and fearful look. When I arrived for the weekend, I would reverse the process: open the intake valve, close the faucets, turn on the water heater. This process theoretically prevented the pipes from freezing while the cabin was empty.

But if the line outside the cabin was frozen, there was little to do. I tried, though. I bought bales of hay and piled them on top of the "spring"—which turned out to be an aluminum-sided hole in the ground covered with a piece of plywood. I spent hours and hours crawling around under the cabin, lying on the icy, muddy ground, recklessly aiming hair dryers at exposed pipes and at the place where the water line emerged from the frozen ground. Finally, when none of these tactics worked, I bought a hatchet and tromped down to the stream with it and some buckets. With my little hatchet I'd ax a hole in the ice, ladle out water to fill my buckets, and stagger back to the cabin. There I'd empty the buckets into a large garbage can bought specifically for that purpose. It was a foolproof system, only very, very inconvenient.

PEACE AND QUIET

WHEN I FIRST bought the cabin, I envisioned it as a place to find peace and quiet and gain insights and new perspectives on life. At the time, I had solitude to spare in Cambridge, and I hoped that in Vermont it would feel different: solitary, rather than antisocial and lonely. That was when I took out all the bunk beds, made room to move in an old upright piano, and prepared to do what I thought was appropriate in my little getaway: read good books, practice my piano, meditate on the beauty of the place, get my head together, finally try to figure out my life. Thank God, I also had a phone.

Looking back, I find that most of my weekend memories are of wintertime. True, wintertime is half the year here, what with preparation for and recovery from the dismal cold. Still, I am surprised that I have to struggle a bit to remember warm sun, green earth, long days. What I remember most is driving up and immediately facing the problem of the water. Will the water run? Have the pipes frozen? Will I remember how to turn on the water? Will I remember not to try to turn on the water until the cabin is warm enough? Or will the water freeze instantly as soon as it enters the pipes, assuming, of course, that it enters the pipes at all?

Then the long weekend would stretch out before me, with or without water, to be filled in all sorts of creative and sustaining ways. Or not. Sometimes I read, or practiced my piano. Sometimes, depending on the weather, I'd spend the weekend shoveling my car out and getting water from the stream. And sometimes I'd spend the time wondering what I was doing there. I'd huddle around my heater, drink wine, smoke cigarettes, filling up the hours until it was time to go back. I made many long-distance phone calls. In some ways, it wasn't all that different from how I spent my weekends in Cambridge.

But even if I didn't achieve true inner peace, it certainly was quiet. I was used to constant background noise: cars, sirens, bells, whistles, radios, televisions, voices, shrieks, and barks. A hardened city dweller, I tuned most of it out. In Vermont, I found a whole new world of sound within the quietness and would become ultrasensitive on my weekends alone.

The cabin is not that far from the next house, maybe the equivalent of five city blocks, but it seemed like a lot of space around me, and I saw it as my boundary. The sound of voices, the occasional person walking past my house down the road, would startle me. I could, and did, count the number of cars that drove by on Sunday afternoons: five, or sometimes seven. I could hear the bells of the village church, a mile or more away. I listened as trees outside let loose their load of snow, branches swishing up, mounds of snow thumping down on more snow. I spent one evening listening curiously to a sweet gurgling sound. Was the brook taking a new route? Was the ditch overflowing? Was it raining somewhere? It turned out that I'd neglected to close a valve behind the toilet when I'd turned the water on; it was as if I'd left a faucet open, and by morning, my well was drained dry.

The sound of true rain was lovely in and of itself; I listened to it pound on the roof, slosh down the walls, and slosh on the ground, and I'd rejoice in my dryness. At night I'd hear animals running across the roof, and probably inside the roof as well. I'd wonder what it was; I didn't yet grasp the extent of the mouse population. In the morning I'd hear chickadees, even though I didn't yet recognize their call. I thought I could hear electricity; the refrigerator, at least, was deafening. When night fell, I heard the darkness grow.

I was feeling lost in life, adrift and at sea. I'd lie in bed and stare up through the skylight at my little patch of sky, as if maybe I could pinpoint my exact location by the stars and by the slight sounds around me. I'd listen. Lily, of course, heard far more than I did. She recognized the ordinary noises for what they were and sorted through them in her sleep, but she could go from deep snores to full attention in a heartbeat. She'd raise her head in the middle of the night, hackles bristling, and softly growl at the dark windows; I'd reach out for her, heart thumping, and time would stand still.

One night I heard it too: an eerie gabble of distant wailing, desolate and heartbreaking and very beautiful. At first I thought it must be a flock of geese lost in some migratory loop, sobbing into the wind as they wheeled in circles high above my cabin. Then somehow I knew it was coyotes. It was their far-off cries and howls traveling down the narrow valley, echoing back and forth off the bare hillsides, dying and dividing through the cold, cold air.

LILY

OF COURSE, I was never all alone. When I tell my dog that she is my angel, as I often do, I mean it quite literally. In many ways she is more familiar to me than anyone or anything else on earth, and she has filled my life with great affection, guarding and protecting me with her love. I suppose she could be any old dog, and I'd love her back just the same. But there she is, who she is, and however I look at her she is a major part of my life. This is by no means the first tribute I have written to her.

I got her ten years ago. I was trying to stop smoking and felt terrible and bereft. A good friend, meaning to distract me, suggested that I get a dog. I thought I realized in a flash of nicotine deprivation that all I wanted was a puppy, that all I needed was just one. No matter that I had just moved to a new apartment managed by an uncompromising cat-owner who had made me promise that I would never get a dog. I thought that if I just bought a small enough dog, no one would notice. My thinking was a bit hazy.

So two weeks later I just went out and bought her. She comes from a particularly disreputable pet store in a mall. I saw her one night; she looked resigned and gloomy in her cage, and she was very little. I threw caution to the winds and, before I could decide not to, charged her on my new MasterCard. I hoped my apartment manager would think she was a cat. I've never told anyone how much she cost.

She is supposedly a purebred cocker spaniel, but most people look skeptical. Even the vet I took her to the next day wasn't sure. He did say that she was definitely a runt, probably from a puppy mill, and he told me that she had a heart murmur and a bad case of mites. He implied I'd paid too much for her, whatever the sum had been. But I didn't care: she was mine, and that was all that mattered.

She certainly doesn't look purebred. She just looks like herself: small and black and somewhat stout, with an unmistakably dogged demeanor. When she runs across the yard to check the compost heap each day, it can best be described as a galumph. Her long, heavy ears flop up and down, as if she were trying to take off, albeit awkwardly, into the wind. Her paws look enormous, but it's all fur. In the fall she gathers clumps of burrs; in the winter her legs and belly are all snow-balled. In the summer she is covered with mud from the pond in the neighboring field. She is always messy.

Food (and drink) is a very big deal with her. She likes to kick her dish around both before and after a meal, and she will bark vigorously at a bottle of beer. Since Amelia arrived and learned to throw her food about, Lily has taken up a military pose in front of the high chair during mealtimes. She sits stock-still, looking up fervently, shifting her weight only occasionally from side to side. When she does not get the food that everyone else is getting, she assumes a sincere and sorrowful expression that makes her look rather like Ronald Reagan, but I still love her. She also very occasionally looks uncannily like Donald Duck.

When she lies down now, it is often with a small grunt; at ten years, she is starting to be an old dog. We often sit together under the nearest apple tree, on the set of steps I moved there from the cabin's back door when the first addition was put on. Sometimes she will lean all her weight against me, perfectly content, asking for nothing more. Other times she likes to have her ears tugged and the furrow between her eyes smoothed down. When I do this, she groans deeply with pleasure. She is a creature, after all, and she loves her comforts.

And yes, she is comforting in return; I lean on her often, too. Even at the lowest of times and even when I am at my very worst, Lily stubbornly, if a little dim-wittedly, continues to sit by my side, and for this I thank her for ever and ever. I take her with me everywhere I possibly can; if for some reason I must leave her behind, I hate it as much as she does.

Before I got her, I had no idea how to begin to measure out my life, or how to think about what a life spanned. Or, to put it more abruptly, how to think about death. She has given me one context, though I now have others, too. Her life is part of mine; may she live many, many more good years with me.

As I write this, I am sitting with Lily on the sofa. She has clambered onto my lap, and so I use her rather broad back to rest my notebook on. Although Amelia greets her with whoops of joy and whole handfuls of Cheerios, my dog is relieved to have me to herself when my daughter goes to bed. At the moment, Lily is happily chewing out perfectly round pieces from what remains of an old army blanket I gave to her many years ago. She spits out each piece expertly, *phphtt, phphtt,* onto the floor. It reminds me of smoking, which I finally did give up some time ago.

After so many years together, you might well think we

could have nothing more to learn from each other. Actually, however, my elderly, small, and stout black spaniel continues to teach me what matters, over and over, day by day. Love, ordinary love, is its own reward. And so, while I suppose she could very well be any old dog, I know she is in fact my angel, watching over me, all spirit, showing me the way.

FURNISHINGS

IT WASN'T ONLY the semiseclusion and the simple beauty of the place that attracted me every weekend. It was also the interior of the cabin, with its simple lack of clutter. I left behind a lifetime's accumulation each time I left Cambridge for Vermont. The cabin was very small, and I managed to keep it relatively sparely furnished at first. It was a relief not to have so much stuff around, and I found I didn't miss any of it. In Vermont, I had only the essential comforts, and they were all essential. In my cabin, everything mattered. It kept the place in focus.

The first things I brought up were among my favorite things.

• One square oak table. I'd had it for almost twenty years. It is the only piece of furniture that I actually did refinish among the several that I intended to. It was painted black when I bought it for ten dollars, and I somehow got all the black paint off. Then I sanded it and put some kind of furniture polish on it that instantly turned it almost black again, which wasn't what I expected. It looks far more solid than it actually is. In fact, it is quite wobbly. It reminds me a bit of Lily, and I love it.

• One possibly cherry rocker, with an old, faded velvet cushion and springs. As soon as I moved it up, the mice burrowed into it from below and dragged out all its stuffing, which turned out to be real horsehair. I'm still meaning to get it reupholstered. It's in the basement now.

• One futon sofa bed. It was the age of futons, and I couldn't yet admit to myself that I found them excruciatingly uncomfortable, both to sit on and to lie on. I piled it high with thick, cheap sleeping bags as a bed. I avoided it altogether as a sofa, and still do.

• An assortment of old wooden chairs, all on their last legs, all now in the basement too.

• Four of my eight Fiestaware plates.

• My early and, to me, beloved attempts at pottery: one extremely heavy plate, a number of surprisingly large bowls, and three mugs whose bases are so thick that it is virtually impossible to tip them over.

• Many yard sale items, collected bit by bit on weekends. They include one interesting electric clock whose numbers would fall like dominoes, losing forty minutes each day; many jelly jars, bought to serve as glasses; an assortment of cutlery—odd forks and spoons, sharp knives with broken handles, spatulas beginning to rust with flaky paint on their real wooden handles; a series of old toasters, each with its own unaccountable foible, including one that would cause each piece of bread to burst into flames and then fling it far across the room, like a blazing meteor; a motley of pots and pans and a separate, unrelated motley of lids. Most of these items are also now in the basement, waiting for the yard sale we plan to have each year ourselves.

- Two throw rugs.
- Brand-new food and water dishes for Lily.
- One very old upright piano. I had a lovely rebuilt baby grand in Cambridge, and I'd found the upright to have something to practice on in Vermont, but it was almost unplayable. I sold it when I moved up with my other piano.
- One old violin.
- One bookcase.
- One black-and-white TV.
- One bureau, perhaps mahogany, but I had only par-

tially stripped only one of its five drawers. Three of the other drawers were painted black, and the last one, a light green. This is in Amelia's room now.

- One small and very old refrigerator.
- Three buckets.
- One large trash barrel for water.
- New garbage pail with secure, mouse-proof lid.

Perhaps I will stop here. Perhaps this sounds like a lot of stuff after all, but some of the items were quite small. Please note, too, that many of them fit into or onto others.

MY FATHER'S VIOLIN

NOW HERE IS Amelia, sitting on my lap while I play the piano. When she first arrived, at five months old, I'd hold my arms close around her to keep her safe from sideways tumbles; to do this, I'd have to transpose most music inward to the octaves around middle C. This limited my repertoire quite a bit, but coincidentally, the same Bach prelude that my father used to play for me lay naturally around her small body, and so I played it often for her, and still do. When she is a few years older, I will bring out my father's violin, open up the case for her, and show her the treasures inside. I know she will like to see it; she loves boxes of all kinds. And maybe she will want to learn to play it. Maybe I'll finally get it fixed up, and maybe she will play with me.

MY FATHER GAVE me his violin fifteen years ago. I asked him for it; I'd always considered myself the musical heir of the family. I had just begun playing chamber music, and I thought I'd take good care of it, find a violinist, form a duo. But instead I put it away next to an old sewing machine and boxes of old books.

When I first got my cabin in Vermont, I brought it up and stashed it in the closet space I'd made with the up-turned bunk beds. I'm not sure why. My father was already ill then; maybe I thought it was important to keep the violin where my heart was. Maybe I knew already that the cabin would become my home. Anyway, the closet was an appropriate home for the violin; he had always kept it on the top shelf of his closet in all the houses our family had lived in through my childhood. He told my sisters and me that he had stopped playing it when college or medical school had taken up too much of his time. He'd never picked it up again, but he couldn't bear to part with it either. It had always fascinated me; I loved the worn leather on the outside of the case and the soft silver velvet of the interior lining. I loved rubbing the bits of old amber rosin, balancing the frayed bow, holding up the violin itself, such an elegant, fragile, light instrument, so very difficult to play.

I have few childhood memories of my father. He was always working, came home late, often returned to his lab or office in the evening. Over the years, my father divided

his lives, settled into priorities. I know he loved his children, but his world was often somewhere else, and we
didn't get to know each other very well. When I grew older,
I felt lucky to have music as a bond; it was something
to fall back on in conversation, and when conversation
flagged, a welcome refuge. We'd give each other birthday
and Christmas presents of Bach and Beethoven, Brahms
and Mahler, put them on, turn up the volume. You do what
you can, and sometimes you connect.

Once, when I was in college, he telephoned me with his
latest discovery, Schubert's piano trios. Schubert's music is
sometimes like memory itself, played through in every
shade of light and dark. The repetitions shift from mode to
mode, breaking your heart over and over, spinning themselves out for as long as they need to, which is often a very
long time indeed. I sat on the floor of my dormitory room,
and hundreds of miles away, my father sat in his big armchair in my parents' living room. Together we listened to the
whole recording; he told me later it was a full thirty dollars' worth of long-distance call. It was one of the few he'd
ever made to me; I remember clinging to the phone, strain-
ing to hear the distant strains of music, wishing there was
something I could say to my own father, wishing he could
talk to me. Maybe he knew how inutterably, speechlessly

confused I was in those times; maybe he didn't. The Schubert was very beautiful. You do what you can, you give and you take what you can.

When I realized that we might have, I was sorry that we'd never played chamber music together, my father and I. I'd started my piano lessons early on, had a modicum of talent and determination. How could we have missed such an easy, natural opportunity for a shy father and daughter who shared a love of music?

But although my father never played his violin, he would occasionally sit down at the piano. I'd sometimes stand behind him or sit next to him on the bench; he'd be lost in the music, playing for himself, but since I was there too, he also played for me. He would have been much too shy to perform for anyone though, as all he knew were two fragments. One was the theme from the third movement of Brahms's Third Symphony, and the other was the opening to Bach's Prelude in C Major from *The Well-Tempered Clavier.*

In my mind, in my memory, these two pieces are the balance of musical expression. My father would pick them out anew each time by ear, listening carefully, eyes almost closed, feeling his way in the dark for the next note. Sometimes he'd seem to stumble upon it unexpectedly, and suddenly, there would be the G, loud and clear. Other times he would just barely brush by the edges of the note, an F, perhaps, then almost miss the corners of the D. Sometimes there would be a searching, almost yearning pause, as if he stood in the middle of the room, arms outstretched, reaching out to catch at the next phrase and let it free again. He would hum along, waiting for his hands and fingers to find their way, and the music was always interesting to me, a rediscovery each time.

When I realized that I might have, and needed to, it was too late to thank him for this way of hearing things. I'd learned to listen in this way; I wish I'd told him so. I wish I'd told him many things.

I IMAGINE NOW, it's all I can do, that my father takes down the violin case from its place on the top shelf of the closet. He frowns at it a little as he opens it—maybe he worries that his daughter will be disappointed in his playing. After all, he did overstate the case a bit when he alluded to the Mendelssohn concerto, telling me casually that he'd often played it in high school. He also told me once that he'd canoed the whole length of the Mississippi River. I want to tell him that it doesn't matter if he misses notes or if he's out of tune. How can I explain?

He takes out the violin, holding it cautiously, as if it might fall to pieces in his hands, like an old pressed flower, but it doesn't. Violins are surprisingly sturdy instruments. I imagine he might feel self-conscious as he tucks the violin under his chin, stretches his right arm once or twice, then takes the bow.

I know that we should start with something easy, but recklessly we choose a movement from a Bach sonata. Beginning it is awkward; who gives the cue? The daughter with conservatory training, or the father with the violin? We trust to luck, start anyhow, and then we're off.

GOLDILOCKS AND
THE THREE BEARS

OCCASIONALLY, I WOULD come up to the cabin
and find someone had been there before me. I learned to
recognize the signs of trespassers. The vast expanse of vir-
gin snow, sullied by someone else's footprints—someone
had walked through my yard! Someone had tromped
down my hill! Tire tracks in my driveway—someone had
parked there! Someone was *still* parked there! I knew
exactly how the three bears must have felt. I wasn't sure,
however, how to handle this new distress. It wasn't that
anything was vandalized or damaged or stolen. No one
actually entered my cabin. I wasn't even there most of the
time. Why should it matter?

I was a new landowner, on unfamiliar ground. I considered myself as respectful as the next person; I didn't peer
through people's windows or walk unbidden through their
front yard. But then, I did take walks with Lily all the time,

through woods, across fields, down streams, over hills. I was cautious during hunting season; otherwise I didn't give it a second thought. Clearly, though, I was on someone else's land most of the time. Why should it not matter?

I took many long drives with Lily, deliberately losing myself on the crisscrossing dirt roads. One fine day in early November we stopped on a long, quiet road in uncharted territory. It was a perfect afternoon for a walk, and this was beautiful Vermont countryside: overgrown pasture-land with unexpected natural clearings, luminous birch groves, dark stands of huge hemlock trees, and rows of old maples following the old boundaries of the fields. Here and there were a few old farmhouses, a few vacation homes and family camps, but not many. We cut across a field and right away discovered, to my amazement, a dried-up pile of moose dung. Thrilled and excited, I followed what I hoped was a moose path through the woods, eyes glued to the ground in search of more evidence of wildlife. Lily raced in circles through the underbrush, following her own trails. And so we almost walked into the cabin's walls before we saw it; honestly, we were almost on its doorstep before we knew it.

It sat right on the edge of one of those unexpected clearings. Its exterior was unpainted barn board; it blended into the background of trees. The front door and porch faced the long view across the field. There was an outdoor grill that had clearly not been used for months. The place was quiet and deserted. I could easily tell that its owners used it as a hunting cabin, and here it was, unoccupied, still out of season for anything.

We were already there, I thought; surely it would be okay just to look. Maybe I'd get some ideas for the cabin. The porch, for instance, was nice and solid and plain, with a built-in bench along one side that looked quite comfortable. The outside grill, too, was well built. I poked around a bit, checked out the bench and the grill, and sat on the front steps with Lily in the lovely sun.

It seemed a perfect spot, and we could have stayed for hours in the unseasonably warm and quiet air. But the slightest of breezes lifted, and I heard something move behind me. When I turned around I saw that the front door was just a bit ajar. It creaked on its hinges in the wind. How odd and interesting, I thought, avoiding the word *scary*. The pull was irresistible, I was helpless. I was up the stairs, I was across the porch, I was at the door. I pushed it open.

It was one small room inside with a dusty woodstove, a table and chairs, a gun cabinet, a sleeping loft, and a rock-

ing chair over by the window in the sun. And in the rocking chair, just waking up, was a woman. She was about my
age, looked respectable and rather nice. She got to her feet,
stricken. I couldn't believe how wrong I'd been. The place
was inhabited, after all.

I was so ashamed that it was almost unbearable. I began
a confused and mortified litany of excuses, from the heart.
I babbled something about the fine day, the long walk, the
unexpected clearing, the open door, how very sorry I was,
I had thought I should check the open door but obviously
it was a terrible mistake, I was so very sorry to intrude. I
probably said something about the moose, too.

But the woman wasn't listening, as I realized when I
finally stopped talking. She, too, was babbling. The open
door, the fine day, the long walk, the rocking chair. She'd
just peeked in to check on the place, and there it was, the
rocker that looked just like her grandmother's. See? Even
the scrollwork on the arms, even the cushion was the same.
It was so odd to see it here—it brought back so many
memories. She remembered how much she had loved sitting in it, how comforting it was, not too little, not too big.
Just right. The long walk must have tired her out more
than she realized, to fall asleep like that. She had never
even known the cabin was here, though she must have

passed this way many times. She and her husband owned that vacation home we'd passed a mile or so back. She had never done anything like this in her whole life. It was completely out of character.

I believed her. In fact, the rocking chair looked a lot like my grandmother's too. The room was peaceful and inviting; it reminded me of home, wherever that might be. I could very well have been in her shoes, coming out from under some strange spell. I could probably just as well have been the one found napping in someone else's seat. I hope I tried to reassure her of all this, but I'm afraid I was just very relieved that it was she, not I, who had got there first. It was bad enough being the one to wake her up.

Anyway, finally, we got it straight. We recognized each other, kindred spirits caught out in an odd coincidence, and then we parted ways, hoping never to meet again.

ROCK BOTTOM

MEANWHILE, I WAS still the tenant in Cambridge, and the building where I'd lived for several years was sold to an enterprising and very extended family. To my outrage, they evicted me; they wanted my unit for their son's new family. I should have seized the moment and used the opportunity to change my life around. But instead I rented yet another run-down apartment on the other side of town.

It was not a good move. In winter the wind blew right through the walls of this new place and rattled through the windows, and the ancient boiler was an ineffective mass of cracked asbestos. The only warm place in the whole apartment was the bathtub, and that is where I spent all and every evening. My world closed in and shrank around me, and the hot water always ran out. This wasn't where I'd meant to land. This wasn't progress.

From this unhappy perspective, I faced my life: it was

not a reassuring sight. I examined in close detail the smooth walls of the bathtub, the high walls of the deep rut I was in; I searched for a way out, but there seemed nothing to hold on to. Cold and dank and badly in need of renovation, in a neighborhood I didn't like, my apartment seemed a reflection of myself; I considered my life, crumbling about me in ruins, as I grew ever more depressed and depressing and regretful. The word *bitter* hung in the air, and *failure* flashed in neon lights nearby. I am sure there were good things too, some of them very good; life was not completely empty or totally awful. But overall, it was a crisis, and I should have seen it coming long before.

I was doing miserably at my job, developing an unmistakably bad attitude. I was a lousy office manager. I could barely bring myself to open my own mailbox, let alone my mail, and they expected me to date-stamp every bill and piece of correspondence? My kitchen table was piled high with fluttery bits of paper, and they wanted me to file? I had long since stopped answering my phone at home, and they still expected me to take their messages? And why couldn't they buy their own pencils? These were far from the right questions, but I asked them anyway. I wailed to myself in despair: Why had I wasted so many years?

My personal life was faring no better; I was not good

company, not a very good friend. I thought I had a monopoly on loneliness. I watched as other people got on with their lives; I felt left behind, abandoned and alone in my little bathtub. I leaned rather heavily on Lily during this period.

Of my many regrets, one of the biggest was that I'd had no children. I was in my forties; it was almost too late. Like many other single women my age, I had begun to look into adoption programs but hadn't taken any steps. Now, however, it seemed that immediate and drastic measures were appropriate, even necessary. In a rush for a quick solution to everything, I signed up with an adoption agency and went through the application process in record time, pretending to myself and everyone else that I knew what I was doing.

Instant family, a ready-made sense of purpose and direction, was what I sought. But this was real, permanent, irrevocable responsibility, and another person's life, and I was very scared. I had no home and no security to offer a small child. Filled with dread, I backed out at the very last minute; I'd even gotten my referral and had bought my plane ticket. It was another false start. I had reached rock bottom and was still going down.

Badly shaken, I cast about for other drastic measures.

To my co-workers' undisguised relief, I decided that I'd finally quit my job, start over, go someplace else. I was lucky not to have to start from scratch. I already had a place to move to: Vermont, I hoped through all my desperation, would be a change that was not too little, not too big, but just right. Lily would be happier there, too. I started work on a small addition to the cabin so that I'd have room to turn my life around.

THE PITS

JULIAN TOOK A photograph of me years ago that is one of the few I like. I am standing by a huge, deep, and very muddy hole. All around me are mountains of dirt. The ground is bare and brown, the trees are bare and gray, and the air looks clammy and cold. A Vermonter might recognize in this scene the season of renewal, and rejoice in the New England spring. I, however, look disconsolate, with perhaps a touch of resigned irony; I also look quite thin, which is probably partly why I like this picture of me. I am standing at the very spot where my cabin, my own dear cabin, had once balanced bravely on its cinder blocks. In its place is now only this hole.

At the time of this photograph, I was sure that I had ruined the prettiest place I'd ever imagined owning. I should have left it alone, not tried to turn it into something more than it should be. I'd already partly spoiled the cabin only the year before, painting it what turned out to be the color of raw liver in a misguided attempt to make it look like a small red barn. Now I was thinking to turn it into a permanent home, perhaps, putting a full-size basement under my one-room Boy Scout cabin. It was a ridiculous, excessive plan.

But I'd done it. A few cold and rainy weekends before, a team of men with steel beams and pulleys and cranes had literally swung the cabin off its precarious feet and out into the back woods, all in one day's work. There it sat on piles of railway ties, peering out from the trees in dismay, its power disconnected, its plumbing severed, its phone line dangling from a poplar tree up the hill.

I had decided to add a small room on to the back. So a foundation crew had excavated this huge pit, big enough for cabin and addition. It was the wettest hole they'd ever seen, they said. They would have to add gravel and dig trenches and put in a whole complex of pipes and drains before they could even think about pouring concrete. They had hit an underground stream; the dirt was pure clay. It was a perfect pond site, they said.

The day of my first glimpse of this disaster I'd had two miserable job interviews for two awful jobs I did not want and would not get. I had also received an unjust and expensive speeding ticket. Then I'd driven three hours to survey my new basement, only to see this dismal pit filling slowly up with water, and all around a mess of mud. I barely recognized my little piece of earth; my lovely week-end haven seemed gone forever. Julian, who visited the following day, tried to reassure me. But later he admitted he'd been shaken, too.

And the size of the addition I'd planned! Its foundation space was carved out the back of this wet cellar hole like an afterthought, the odd scoop of the shovel, a mistaken notch. I saw it for what it would be: a pitiful, vestigial, stingy little ell poking uselessly off the end of the little cabin. For this I'd hacked away, flooded, and clogged the only bit of level ground in the four acres I owned. It was not worth it. It was a tiny, terrible plan.

I was depressed. The whole project seemed only an exercise in futility, and futility was something I thought I had already mastered. I did not need this horrible hole to tell me any more.

Anyway, there I am, rueful and thin in this photograph that despite everything I still rather like. My hands are in my pockets, my shoulders hunched a bit; my head is bowed. I'm looking at my new-dug pit; I stare into its depths, heart sinking as I wonder what I've done. As far as I can see, it's just a sea of mud. It's not yet clear to me that right there, right at my feet, lies the foundation of my future.

THE FIRST ADDITION

Room to Live In

THE BASIC FRAMEWORK

SECRETLY, I WISHED for a three-story tower that would lift me above the hilltops and show me the open sky above. As a more sensible and affordable alternative, however, I thought a single, simple room should suffice. I chose a dimension at random, rather like choosing a rug size. "A room twelve by twenty, please," I told the builder I had hired. And so, there was the basement hole, followed in due course by the basement itself. The cabin was retrieved and lowered gently onto its impressive foundation. The twelve-by-twenty room was to fit onto the back, making an ell.

It was indeed a tiny amount of space, after all, for all my stuff and my piano too. The builder agreed. He said he could cantilever it so that it would stick out over the foundation two feet, making the final dimensions fourteen by twenty. I had the idea to have a loft for my bed, forgetting that Lily would not be able to climb a ladder and that I myself was quite terrified of heights. The builder agreed it could be done; it would just cost a bit more. At the very last minute, the loft space grew to half a story, with a short four-foot knee wall and a real set of stairs.

To offset the added expense of the second story, I bargain-hunted for the windows myself, and that explains, to anyone who wonders, why there is such a variety. It never occurred to me to plan for consistency; I bought whatever was cheapest. Out of ten windows, there are six different sizes and brands, and the glass door is of another ilk altogether.

The best finds were two windows that Julian and I found at a building salvage place. They had been custom-made for an exotic mansion in New Hampshire, subsequently dismantled. They are an odd size, long and narrow, divided into smaller square hinged sections. The glass is triple paned, the wood is a heavy, dark mahogany, and the sections open smoothly and then close just the way I imagine a really expensive car door would close. *Thunk,* and the sound of a latch catching, and the thing is shut, draft-free, secure, solid, dependable, closing after closing. The carpenters framed these windows horizontal and low, like portholes in the knee walls of the second story. The other windows were a conventional assortment of sale items from different building supply places. They were just good deals. More or less at random, the same way I bought them, I finally chose places for them all in the walls.

Any savings I might have achieved in the overall cost by buying the windows myself, however, was spent in the short time it took me to draft a note to the carpenters. I came up after the framing was completed and thought I realized how unbearably claustrophobic my initial design had been. I redesigned my walls, then wrote the following request and tacked it to the stairs.

"Dear Carpenters," it began.

"It looks so wonderful, thank you very much. I just had an idea about the windows. Could you separate the two on the hill side, first floor, and put the taller one that is currently on the second floor, north side, in between them? Here is a smaller window I just bought to go in that bigger one's space. [Arrow pointing down to the new window below.] Also, here is a small octagonal window I found for the peak of the roof. It was only $25! [Another arrow pointing to the other new window.] And then I thought maybe the window on the road side, first floor, could exchange places with the smaller one on the back side, also first floor. And could that back window be shifted just a few feet over to the left? Then the hill side walls would look like an enclosed porch, I thought. Anyway I really really apologize for asking for these changes now. I hope it's possible to do and not too much trouble. And thank you!!! for everything. It really does look great." The note was illustrated by a very complicated diagram.

They did it all. I never could bear to figure out exactly how much the changes cost, but it probably took them one full day and possibly two to reframe the walls. The tiny twenty-five-dollar octagonal window required repositioning half of the roof rafters as well; it looks a bit silly in the shallow peak, but I like it anyway. The hillside "porch" was a strange idea since it looks directly onto a steep incline, not the most majestic of views. It is actually a nice effect, however, at least in the summertime. When you enter the room from the opposite side, all you can see out the impressive expanse of window is a wall of green grass, fifteen feet away.

It was hard for me to consider the project from anyone else's perspective, though the carpenters seemed really to care how it all came out. They did all the work, but I felt far more overwhelmed. To me, it was an enormous and terrifying undertaking, fraught with agonizing indecision every step of the way. To them, it was just a simple three or four days' work, complete with a few aggravations. The place felt kind of lonely when they left.

HOPE AT THE BEGINNING

MY MODEST ADDITION, even in its final two-room version, didn't include a separate child's room. But I hadn't given up on motherhood. I figured I'd give myself a year, see where I was then, and maybe try again.

I'd had good reasons not to go ahead with the adoption; for that matter, though, I'd always had good reasons not to have a child. For a long time I'd considered myself too young, too immature, too underemployed, my relationship, when there was such a thing, too shaky. Then, before I knew it, I was too old as well. This reasoning was not unfamiliar; I'd applied it regularly over the years to any major step that presented itself. Change had become increasingly difficult with time, opening up like an ever wider and deeper chasm, requiring an ever longer running start to take off in a terrifying leap of faith.

Still, despite nightmarish fears and reservations, when

I'd turned forty I found I wanted desperately to have a baby. If I looked for reasons, they were probably the same ones many women have. I didn't want to miss another of life's passages. I wanted to love a child and a child to love. I hoped for a new connection to the future, a new understanding of the past, a new responsibility, and a role in life.

I daydreamed a lot, tried to picture her, my child, and me, her mother. My daughter would of course look like me, like one of the few pictures I have of myself as a child, serious and pudgy and intent on a shoelace, or a bucket, or whatever task might be at hand. We'd eat breakfast together at my old kitchen table, the morning sun slanting in the windows—these scenes were sometimes rather misty and unrealistic, with long windswept views, cornflakes and fresh biscuits on the table, sparkling-clean floors. She would be defiant, while I would be patient; we would have cheerful arguments. We'd get through hard times, whatever they might be, together. We'd be a good family. She'd have a little bike, and I'd help her off down her first wobbly ride. Maybe she'd like a real pogo stick, and a bongo board, too. I'd be sensibly strict about TV and video games; I had boxes of my favorite childhood books stored away for her to read.

I remembered the old songs my mother adapted for our

dog, a beloved and determined dachshund. "Mighty Like A Rose" was one of several. I myself had a growing repertoire of songs in praise of Lily, and I was ready to teach them all to my own small child. We'd sing together in the car. We'd explore the world.

When I'd first thought of adoption I was driving back to Boston from a weekend in Vermont. This was years ago, long before I'd moved. It was late in the day and the sun was behind me. The afternoon light streamed across the earth sideways, illuminating the air itself rather than the land, and leaving a long, shadowy path over the high hills. It was really like a ray of hope: suddenly I saw a solution to the cycles of disappointment and obsessions with fertility that had taken over my life. I would adopt a child; it seemed so very simple at that moment. In the end it was a long and difficult path, with that awful first false start and more roadblocks and pitfalls to come. I needed a long running start indeed, and it was a truly terrifying leap of faith to take. But I like remembering that there was this light at the beginning.

AND I HEAR Amelia now. Here she is, aged two and a half, sitting in the backseat of the car, commenting on her own world as the country views unfold outside her window.

"Maybe we'll see a garbage truck?" she asked me wistfully the other day, as we started a drive through some of the loveliest countryside of New England. After a full hour of uninterrupted beauty, she drew her own conclusions. "You know what, Mommy? Sometimes I'd like a goldfish," she announced with a serious nod. To my great satisfaction, she has just started to sing to Lily. Her favorite song is "Happy Birthday." Her Chinese name is PanPan. It means "hope."

HEAT, PART ONE

WHEN THE CARPENTERS had finished their work and I'd run out of bank loan, I had a solid, beautifully built structure. Obviously, though, a lot was missing: Lights, I recognized dimly when night fell. Heat, walls, et cetera. Everything. I stood in the middle of the room and looked around at bareness. All the many things I'd always taken for granted as being in a room were lacking in my new addition. The outside was another matter altogether. I'd never even thought to wonder how a house worked. I learned there is a logical sequence to putting a room together; each step of the way was new. I learned a lot from my mistakes, some little, others not so small.

Julian was interested, offering suggestions, extending help that I happily accepted. He said the electric and phone wires should go in at the beginning, and in short time he'd wired the whole addition and installed my precious phone jacks. His work was delicate and precise; he handled needle-nose pliers and tiny strands of wire and stubby, short screws with complete ease, as if they were extensions of his fingers, as if he were just sitting at a table writing a letter or eating lunch. It didn't seem to bother him, working at odd angles in dark corners of ceilings and walls. He planned out circuits for wall plugs and ceiling fixtures, put in two-way switches, knew exactly what he was doing. He explained to me about currents and grounds, circuits and circuit breakers. I tried to help, but the strands of wire would twist and fray and the little screws were always rolling out of sight.

After he'd finished, however, it was my turn; insulation was the next step, and it was something I could do. This was Vermont, and insulation was important. The standard type is quilted fiberglass with brown paper on one side. It comes in big rolls, and you roll it out like toilet paper and slice off appropriate lengths at appropriate angles with a utility knife. You plump these lengths into each bay, stapling the paper edges to the studs with a rather stiff giant stapler; the insulation is supposed to fit snugly but not tightly. Ideally, it is as if the room were encased in a down sleeping bag with lots of loft to trap air; this is what keeps the heat in.

I'd often heard people complain about insulation, and I soon understood why. For whatever reason, the fiberglass is usually pink, sometimes yellow, and looks just like cotton candy, even down to the irregularities in texture and color. I learned quickly that this is a bitter, bitter irony; it is actually quite horrible, insidious and itchy stuff, and shredded bits of insulation get into your mouth and eyes and clothes. I finished quickly, to get it over with. It was not a very neat job, but the walls looked puffy and quilted and warm.

Unfortunately, they only looked that way. Insulation, however warm and comforting it my look, does not actually create heat. It only conserves it, and in our addition there was none to conserve.

Heat was the top priority. I decided to get a woodstove; it would be a simple, thrifty, back-to-basics approach to heat, I thought. This was Vermont, a thrifty, ecologically aware state, and everyone had one. The handsome, high-tech, and very expensive chimney I subsequently purchased was made of sections of brand-new shiny metal asbestos-lined pipe; the man I bought it from attached it with brackets to the back of the addition, on the outside. My hearth was a huge, square slab of slate that took up much of the floor space. It had all become a complicated and major investment.

Fully installed, the stove certainly had its good points. It was indeed very warm, and it smelled nice. With the door open, it was a blazing fireplace; I spent hours watching it. I rediscovered marshmallows and burned my toast. But it took up a lot of space. It had to be positioned just right, a safe distance from the wall in back, and with enough hearthstone in front to safely catch any live ashes or cinders. With the many windows and the stairs, there was only one place that the stove would fit, and there it essentially blocked the back door. Piles of wood took up yet more space in the living room, and the reserve stockpile filled the porch to the brim. It was overwhelming. I'd had no idea. I'd always simply turned a knob to get warm.

It was warm, true, but sometimes too warm. The air felt smothery and smoky sometimes—stifling, in fact. I'd bought a big stove for a little room. I had only just become aware of creosote—a residue that builds up in chimneys, sometimes catching fire, and is more a problem with airtight stoves—and I worried obsessively about it: I couldn't sleep at night, it was so hot, I was so anxious.

It was actually a relief when I realized what a huge mistake I'd made. It was a simple matter of square footage. Before I moved my furniture in, I saw belatedly that a room fourteen by twenty feet could not possibly accommodate both a radiantly hot stove and a large, delicate musical instrument, and I preferred my piano. So I bought some electric heaters and moved the woodstove out to sit in the cold shed, where, years later, it remains. And years later, its expensive bright new chimney still hangs off the back wall, now as an interior oddity in the hallway of the second addition, my shining example of, and monument to, Poor Planning.

WALLS

THE NEXT HURDLE was the walls. I hired two young brothers to hang the sheets of drywall; they did it in a weekend. I decided to do the taping myself; the pictures in the build-your-own-home book I had bought looked so straightforward. You take these long pieces of paper tape and glop them over the seams between the sheets. The glop is drywall compound that looks like plaster and is familiarly called mud, and you spread it in broad, paper-thin layers with wide drywall knives. When it dries, you sand it a bit and apply some more, and sand it a bit, and do that for a few layers, spreading it wide so that there won't be a perceptible ridge. You cover up screws and nail marks in much the same way.

I can do this by myself, I told myself and Julian too, who just nodded with his nicest smile. He'd already done some taping in his youth and was just as glad not to do any more, he said. So I bought a roll of tape, some sandpaper, and two buckets of drywall compound, which the salesmen at the building supply store put in my car. They lifted them in one swift motion, no sweating, no grunting, no oaths. Two buckets fit in the hatchback area; I noticed how the car sank with the new weight.

When I got back to the cabin, however, I found I myself did not have the strength to lift them out of the car. This was a definite obstacle. The buckets took up too much room in the back for me to be able to get in too and try to lift them out from underneath. The back of the trunk was too high for me to just roll them out. I tried using a shovel as a lever and broke the blade right off under the first bucket. I honestly don't remember how I did it; I might have taken the backseat out and rolled them out the door. I do remember resenting bitterly the whole construction industry, so thoughtlessly and brutishly dominated by the male physical frame.

It was a conspiracy of men. These buckets didn't have to be so big and heavy. The staple guns I'd used to put the insulation in didn't have to be so hard to squeeze. Power tools didn't have to be so terrifying, unwieldy and heavy and dangerous all at the same time. I developed a whole new thesis of oppression. I am not particularly weak; it shouldn't have had to take me so long just to get the god-damn buckets out of the car. They could easily sell the stuff in smaller, lighter buckets, but they don't. It isn't right.

Anyway, the taping was much harder than it looked in the pictures and took much longer than I'd expected. I wasn't as good at it as I'd hoped. I'd get flakes of dried-up compound in the bucket and on my knife, and they would scratch deep grooves with every stroke. It was messy, rather torturous work, and I sensed it shouldn't be. It should be like Oriental brushwork, one movement incorporating everything. The hand, the compound knife, the tape, the mud, the wall, the seam, the past, the present, and the future should all move together in harmony, in one long sweeping motion, feathering, tapering off softly in a light and simple gesture. If you fuss at it, God forbid, or try to fix it or, worse yet, try to hurry, you ruin the moment and the intention and make a mess of your wall.

I never did catch on. So, from necessity, I went about it the other way around: I'd pile on a huge mound of lumpy, scratchy mud and then sand almost all of it off. The end result was sort of the same, but not the same at all: deter-mination, not grace. Still, good therapy. My inside walls were all hard-won.

• • •

I'D WAITED UNTIL early spring to quit my job in Boston. I thought it would take me months to find work in Vermont, leaving me more than enough time to thoughtfully finish up the details of my rooms and move my stuff in at my leisure. Unexpectedly, however, I was offered a job that started in three weeks. I was in a tremendous rush, frantic, in two places and in between all at once. I barely had time to worry about how much my life was changing. The previous owner, now my neighbor down the road, was a superb carpenter, and he agreed to trim the many downstairs windows. I painted my new walls a pure and blinding white, shielded my eyes like Dracula against the morning glare, and hastily repainted them a creamier shade. Julian helped me put down a wood floor. It all happened so fast I hadn't had time to appreciate what we were accomplishing. But when the room was done, it was stunning, opening up from the dark and shady cabin, clear and clean and full of light.

It was also in the nick of time. The piano and other furniture I'd not been able to move myself were delivered on Sunday. The next day I began my new job. I'd moved.

SOMEWHERE TO GET TO

> *. . . the sun shone*
> *As it had to on the white legs disappearing into*
> *the green*
> *Water; and the expensive delicate ship that must*
> *have seen*
> *Something amazing, a boy falling out of the sky,*
> *Had somewhere to get to and sailed calmly on.*
> —W. H. AUDEN, "Musée des Beaux Arts"

IT TOOK SEVERAL weeks to unpack and settle in, and by then the weather was warm and the glory of green was everywhere. It was an easy transition from a bleak and unheated apartment to the warmth of my front yard. The world opened up to the outdoors; I took pleasure in the sun, windy skies, clean air. I no longer lived in a bathtub. I stayed outside as much as possible to shake off my old life and used the weekends to explore my new state.

I studied maps at first. I found the Geological Survey map that showed all the details of my immediate vicinity, down to the little dot that is my cabin. Bookstores sold huge atlases of the entire state, dividing it into thirty or forty full-page sections, and I bought one of these as well; to get an overview, I'd check each section with my full-scale road maps. Lily and I were happy just to sit out on my front steps in the summer morning sun as I oriented myself. Sitting there, I'd ramble off in many directions.

I love to study maps, anyway, anywhere. Sometimes even my dreams are maps, taking place in several scales at once. I take a step, over Arizona, say, to the California coastline. Far below I see the outline of all the states, all in different primary colors. Arizona is bright yellow, California green; Mexico is orange and to my left—I can make out the entire country. The Grand Canyon is far below, a deep, wide gash, the rivers squiggly lines; the mountain ridges to my right are in clear relief. Sometimes I bounce lightly over vast expanses of land and water, like a huge balloon; other times I hover, float down low for a closer look at the outlines of cities, parks and houses, fields and interstate routes.

Maybe any abstract logic can impose itself on a sleepy and unsuspecting mind. I've dreamed in harmony and counterpoint exercises, in Dewey decimal, in touch typing and long-distance driving; geography is just another system. At any rate, my map dreams don't always make much sense to me, but they seem to take place in the language of dimensions and perspectives. They certainly have little to do with the fine art of dream-flying, which I cherish, and although I look down from a great altitude, they aren't about heights either. (In those nightmares, I'm frozen against a stairwell wall, unable to move because there are no railings.) I think they might come from moving around so much as a child: I spent a lot of time looking at road and city maps and apartment plans. I came to see this as a way to try to hold on to the world, understand it, fold it up, put it in my pocket, and carry it with me wherever I went.

The Green Mountains are the heart of Vermont and run a clear, straight path north–south through the whole state. The Long Trail is the hiker's path that follows along the entire long, flat ridge, and there is a network of other trails up the bigger mountains to join onto it. I decided I would explore the state on weekends with day trips here and there, and get in shape by taking long hikes in the mountains. Julian joined me too when he could.

By many standards, the Green Mountains would scarcely qualify as foothills, which was fine with me. I'd had little experience hiking—as a rule I avoid heights whenever possible. I'd climbed only one high mountain in my life, and that almost by mistake. I'd lived in Boulder right after college; my first housemates were native Coloradans who had grown up in the Rockies. I stayed in touch, and many years later, when Lily was just a puppy, I went to visit them for a summer vacation. My friends had all just taken up long-distance mountain running; I was still smoking a pack a day. Their healthy summer goal was to climb all the peaks in Colorado over fourteen thousand feet. I went along for one of these climbs when I first arrived; it seemed the thing to do. They said it wouldn't be too hard. We'd start at eleven thousand feet, and it was only a few miles to the top.

The lower part was beautiful. I would have been content to spend the whole day in the clear, high, blue mountain valley, lying in the grass perhaps, perhaps smoking a cigarette or two. I was less and less content, however, the higher we went. Lily was fine, and bounded right along, but I felt the altitude. My arms were tingly and weird; I'd breathe as deeply as I possibly could, but it wouldn't seem to make any difference at all. It was like trying to suck satisfaction from an ultralight cigarette after decades of smoking Marlboros. "This is it? You call this air?" I tried to complain, but had no extra strength for words. Gasping at the elusive wisps of oxygen, it was all I could do to drag one heavy foot after another. I was so exhausted I even forgot about my fear of heights.

But when we reached the summit, fear returned. One side of the peak sheered off in a long, straight drop of a thousand feet or more. The clouds that were racing by below us would hit this cliff, hurtle up its side, and burst over the top in a shower of mist that seemed to crystallize and evaporate at once into the thin, light air. The climbers who were gathered at the top ran over to the edge each time to marvel at this phenomenon. The mountaintop was also famous for lightning, and you could hear the charge gathering.

This was the top of the world: all around were snowy mountains, floating in the sky like clouds, and the sun was hard and bright. I sat in the exact middle, as far away from any edge as possible, encircled by a bejeweled crown of identical crystalline peaks, and listened to the crackling rocks. The earth spun wildly around and topsy-turvy too; maybe I was simply dizzy. I lost my faith in gravity: we'd all be whirled away, go flying off the top of that high mountain, our bodies tossed out to the wind. I couldn't bear to watch my friends leaning over at the edge of nothing. I didn't know what else to do, so I put my jacket over my head, held Lily tightly in my lap, and closed my eyes. I wanted to cry. I'd seen enough. I'll never climb so high again.

The Green Mountains, on the other hand, have few cliffs and plenty of soft moss to land on. They are comforting, rather than overwhelming, in their beauty, with lovely, lowly, flat-topped mountain peaks bathed in the iridescent green of everything. And even if the peaks are not that high, you still feel that you've gotten somewhere when you reach the summit. Lily was in heaven, and so was I. On these weekend hikes, my dreamy sense of cartography would take hold right away, and the long, low ridge would seem to roll out like a welcome carpet at my feet. With no outstanding peaks to go by, Julian would often get confused about which way was north or south, east or west. But I'd be oriented firmly in the third dimension. I'd see the compass points as clearly as if they were written in the sky; up and down were just as obvious. I could point unerringly in the direction of any town or river, lake or highway.

We'd look down, rather than up, at a circling hawk, at the diving swallows making fine adjustments with their wings, disappearing in a sharp angle of flight. Near one mountain there was an aviation club that rented rides in gliders. We'd often watch them aloft on the winds below, lazily buoyed on those long, light wings. They looked so quiet and graceful that we went so far as to find the airstrip and ask the price of a ride, though we went no further than that. Sometimes we'd see a glider catch an updraft and slice up the side of the mountain to circle round the summit. Its wings would cut through the air with an alarming hissing sound, its huge shadow racing over the rocks like that of some enormous bird of prey. From pure instinct, we'd all scatter for a place to hide. I couldn't see the faces of the people flying, but I could well imagine myself sitting in their place, my jacket pulled tightly over my head, my every muscle tensed for imminent disaster.

Julian and I got good at hiking that first summer and became quite cocky. One weekend we started a climb up a familiar mountain on an unfamiliar trail, although we knew it was too late in the afternoon to get back before dark. The weather turned ominous halfway up, and the sky was stormy long before we reached the turn up to the bare-rocked final ascent. The clouds began to settle on the mountain, and somehow we got off the foggy trail. There was a dark glint of metal through the fog and underbrush: we'd stumbled upon the wreckage of a small plane that had crashed many years before. It must have gone down in bad weather, slammed right into the side of the mountain. It was in pieces, but the pieces that were left were still almost intact; I think you could have walked the length of one wingspan and even climbed into the cockpit. Moss had grown over much of it, and trees grew around and through the wreckage; it had become part of the hillside. The place held history; the past was right there. Someone had died there and left behind his dreams. We walked around it for a bit, and then we hurried back down through the rain that had just started to fall. Later I saw it listed in a trail guide as a point of interest, worth making a detour for; we had been drawn to it by accident, but it is indicated with a small sign and a narrow path from the main trail.

Another summer day we stopped along the road to get a sandwich at a convenience store. We'd just parked the car when something amazing in the distance caught my eye. From our perspective on the ground it seemed to me that sticks were falling, lightly, gently, catching the sunlight, right out of the clear blue sky. There was a small airplane too, circling aimlessly down, around and around and around. We watched for a while but could make no sense of it, and so we walked on into the store. When we came outside a bit later we remembered to check the sky again, but there was nothing left to see.

They say that accidents happen in slow motion, and still they catch you unawares. We found out only later that we'd witnessed a crash. There had been an air show that day, small planes and sky divers performing their triumphant stunts in choreographed formations. Then something terrible occurred: one plane tangled with a parachutist, and what I'd thought were sticks were really broken wings and bodies, tumbling through the air. I thought about it for a long time afterward, about what we'd seen, how we'd shrugged in puzzlement, sailed calmly by, and gone on with our day. If we had stood our ground, maybe we'd have recognized the event for what it was, but the accident had been so far away, so casual, no loud explosions or plumes of smoke to mark it as a tragedy. I saw it happen like a dream and could not understand it.

GARDENS

OUR GARDEN STARTED small and was a new beginning, the first thing Julian and I had grown together. The house was an ongoing project, interesting in and of itself, but the garden was different; we began to talk in terms of the next season rather than the coming weekend. In spring, we found ourselves considering future years; there were biennials and perennials to discuss. Before we knew it, we'd planted rosebushes. We were making many plans together, discussing donkeys and pigs, devising ambitious projects involving barns. From time to time I'd bring up the possibility of a child. Gradually, we got used to talking about her.

It was summer. Julian said we should try growing vegetables, but I'd been discouraged; other people's vegetable gardens were so big. It seemed like such a lot of digging to do. Julian said we could start out with a little plot, three feet by four. We could dig it bigger next year, he said. We didn't have to do everything at once. He often suggested taking things a step at a time; this was a concept that was gradually sinking in for me.

And so we chose the spot in the front lawn that seemed to have the most sun, and then we dug out the sod. It looked like a garden right away, even when there was nothing growing in it, when it was just a neat, rectangular patch of bare, brown earth. We squeezed the earth in our hands to determine its texture, as the gardening books suggested. It formed a stiff and unyielding mass; I'd already been told the land was almost pure clay. So we added sand left over from the foundation work to give it some crumbliness and drainage, and next considered mulch and fertilizer. Clearly, cow manure was the answer.

Although there are many cows around Vermont and therefore much manure for the taking, I felt too shy to ask any farmer for their cow dung. To begin with, I wasn't sure how to get it back to the cabin. Where would I put it in my car? In big buckets in the hatchback? Would I be able to get them out again? Then I worried about how to ask how much it cost. Perhaps it was free, and they would laugh at me. Or perhaps I would be expected to offer some predetermined amount. I had no idea what that amount should be, nor, for that matter, did I know how much I needed. I wasn't even sure what to do with it, how much to put on, whether to put it on in the spring or fall, or whether to let it age first. I'd seen plastic bags of composted manure for sale. The word "composted" made me worry further. Should I ask for old, rather than new, manure? Would there be such a thing?

The answers to all these concerns were surely straight-forward. But I didn't know what they were, so I finally just bought bags of expensive preprocessed cow dung, proba-bly from Illinois, at a hardware store chain and dumped them onto the little garden. Julian added lime, we dug it all in, and our first vegetable garden plot was prepared.

The first year, we started off with two rows of spinach and some radishes. And to my astonishment, they grew. The spinach was a bit tough and the radishes rather dry, but it was all edible and very encouraging. We were gar-deners! And so each year we dig our garden out a little big-ger, face the same questions about manure, buy the same plastic bags of processed stuff—though I have now moved up to an even more expensive, local, "organic" blend of dung. I am easily taken in.

We have some odd successes and some disagreements. Arugula and peppermint flourish unexpectedly well, although we are not sure what to do with the mass quantities that grow. I like eggplants; I think they are the most beautiful vegetable of all. Julian thinks that they are unproductive and in general inedible. He likes tomatoes, but I am not impressed by the few that survive the blight, the cold, the cloudiness, the general shortness of summer. As far as I can see, they mostly just get hard and green, and then they rot. We compromise by planting some of each. But we both like our standard crops of lettuce and greens, carrots, peppers, beans, and zucchini. They are dependable and very tasty and need no coddling or special care. They raise no false expectations and present no problems, and it is quite incredible to me to make a meal of anything I grow.

Anyway, after several years of gardens I remain a rank beginner. I barely know the terminology. One weekend Julian excitedly announced there was a volunteer potato plant in the compost. I pretended that I understood, but I learned only later that this was an independent vegetable, a surprising potato that had just decided to grow of its own free will. A neighbor explained to me that the tomato plants were so leggy because the sunlight is limited; I thought I saw what he meant when I studied their long, skinny stalks. I found out about runners from the peppermint, which spreads like a weed, uncontrollably, on long, horizontal root systems. I learn something new every year.

Julian informed me one midsummer weekend that my spinach was bolting. He meant that it had gone to seed, but I didn't know that. I ran to the window. Truthfully, I hadn't gone near the garden in many days. I feared, perhaps hoped, to see the whole garden rebelliously plotting its escape, all our little vegetables drawing themselves up on their long, leggy stalks and sending out their runners, readying to flee the confines of the chicken wire fence we'd strung up for the deer to step over. I could see our zucchinis muddling about in disarray, tripping over their own vines in their sudden haste, tangling themselves up in the long roots of the peppermint. The lettuce and arugula would fly away and the spinach would follow in a short gust of wind; the tomatoes and eggplant would trot briskly along together, scattering their small, hard fruits behind them. The beans would wrap themselves in their leaves and march off in rows. The peppers would scamper, the carrots would hop, and the beets would roll away, and only the neat, rectangular patch of dirt would remain.

FREDDY

I PICKED HIM up partly because I was already late for work. I had a thirty-mile commute, but this was not a good enough excuse for being chronically late to my job. I was trying to make a good impression, but once again I was halfway to work and with seven minutes left to travel the fifteen remaining miles. Then I saw Freddy. He was weaving along the shoulder of the interstate, veering out onto the pavement, looking for a way across. As I watched, the truck in front of me just barely missed him.

So I stopped my car, partly out of fear that he would be run over, and partly because I saw an unusually compelling excuse to be late for work. And partly to try to make amends to an old ghost. A long time ago I'd worked for a research lab that used stray dogs from the pound in their experiments. The first dog they worked on when I was there was a beagle mix. I was a lowly lab assistant, and my job was to take him out for a walk before the experiment began, and I've always been sorry that I didn't simply walk on home with him, quit my job in style, save that nice, silly dog's life. I didn't think the experiments they did were doing anybody any good. But I wasn't brave enough or sure enough, and so I took him back.

This time, at least I stopped my car. He looked like the same dog, and though he was a bit shy, I coaxed him into my car easily enough. He was skinny and caked with weeks of muck, had on an old green collar but no tags, and was evidently lost. As I'd thought, people at work took it well in stride when I showed up with him; they had dealt with far worse emergencies than my dirty and excitable beagle puppy. I kept him under my desk, where he barked all day, and then took him home.

Lily was surprised but at first quite nice about it. He was a fellow dog, after all. He was also starving, his needs obviously so much greater than hers that she actually stood by while he devoured her dinner, stole a loaf of bread off the kitchen table, and ransacked the garbage. I gave him a bath and called everywhere I could think of to try to find his owners, but no one had reported him missing.

The next day was Saturday. Julian came up with his kindly Spot, and Freddy joined our foursome, or at least tried to. But the four of us had achieved a real balance over time. It was clear whose dog or person was whose, and everyone had a place to call their own. We understood how and when to make room for one another. Freddy, however, was everywhere, all at once. It was like having a friendly tornado around. Indoors, he raced in circles, barking ecstatically. Outside he was pure hound. He would catch a scent and follow it wherever it led as if he were being pulled along in its zigzag path, reeled in like a fish on a line to the next scent. He dug up the garden, ran away with shingles in his mouth. He was on the move all day. We fed him all he could eat.

In return, he openly adored us, followed us closely, always underfoot, awkward, falling over himself in inadvertent somersaults, flustered but exuberant. He wanted to sleep on the bed, crawled under the covers, crept up in the middle of the night to sleep on the pillow between our heads.

Lily cooled to him, but Spot was a more tolerant soul, and also large enough to largely ignore him. Julian and I grew more and more fond of him and at the same time more and more anxious. I worried about Lily's feelings; Julian worried that we would never be able to go anywhere ever again. Traveling with two dogs was the limit. Three, especially with a dog like Freddy, was way, way over. It wasn't going to work. We didn't know what we would do.

No one called for him. On Monday I went to work, Julian and Spot went to Boston, and Lily and Freddy were left to themselves and each other in the house. I bought the biggest bag of puppy chow I could find on the way home, figuring I'd better be prepared. When I opened the door, Freddy came flying into my arms, barking nonstop, tail zinging a mile a minute, big smile, soft ears, irresistible dog, much love, little brain. I saw Lily standing back a ways with a look of awe—not one of her standard expressions—on her familiar, stubborn face. Freddy bounced off my chest, and it was then that I noticed little pieces of stuff all over the kitchen floor. They were like pieces of ragged cardboard, only stiffer, and they lay everywhere. I picked one up and realized then that it wasn't little pieces of stuff on the floor; it was the floor itself. Freddy had ripped up the whole linoleum kitchen floor and torn it to shreds. No wonder Lily was impressed.

Shortly after, as if coincidentally, my veterinarian's office called to say they knew who the owners were, and wasn't that wonderful news. I wasn't sure. The problem was solved, though: no more dilemma, no more Freddy, new floor.

So I took him back. It was an assortment of ramshackle buildings, with a cow or two, a goat, a junkyard, and several other dogs. The family was friendly and seemed happy to have him back. He was to be their son's hunting dog. They never let him in the house; they had three house dogs already. His name, of course, was not Freddy. He looked sad when I left; it wasn't where he wanted to be. He'd thought he'd found love in his newfound home.

It felt all wrong to me, too. The next day I returned to his house, bringing my fifty pounds of puppy chow as an excuse to drop by; I wasn't sure what I intended to say. I was too late, though. His family thanked me but told me that he'd run off again. They said they were tired of him running away so much. They told me to keep him, if I ever saw him again. I looked for him for a long time, but I never did see him again.

JOBS

"I WON'T!" I woke myself up shouting many years ago. I was having an employment-related nightmare. "I *won't* sort paper clips for the army!" I found myself bolt upright in my bed. It was a fairly straightforward dream, no great revelation. Actually, at the time, it wasn't paper clips I was sorting and it certainly wasn't for the army. Au contraire. But it was how I often saw my situation.

Right out of college I spent a year in another university town, crowded with supposedly overqualified graduates ready to do anything. I finally landed my first job, putting snaps on sleeping bags and parkas. The workers who blew the down feathers into the presewn sections, women all, made slightly more money than the snappers did. Coincidentally, on the very day I applied for work at the factory one of the featherers burst out of a door, covered in soft, fluffy down from head to toe, wearing a beaklike yellow face mask. She looked like a gigantic baby duck. She was squawking, spitting feathers, quitting in disgust. This was the golden egg, a perfect job opportunity.

But it looked like a bad place, the coop from which she'd flown, so I became a snapper anyway. My supervisor, the Senior Snapper, spent her spare time counting the pounds she was losing as a new weight watcher: eighty-seven at the time I was hired. She kept a running tally along with an updated series of before-and-after photographs on the wall by her snapping machine. It kept her spirits up; they would flag only occasionally, and then she would eat an entire box of peanut butter cookies for lunch. Her husband was getting a doctorate in philosophy. That fact had helped her land this job; the enlightened capitalists who ran the factory saw her as the stabilizing element of their workforce; surely it would take her husband years and years to complete his thesis, and meanwhile they would have his wife, albeit thinner and thinner. Her name was Jane. Plain Jane, she said, and pointed with satisfaction to the latest photo, the slimmest version of an interesting and very funny woman.

She told me that the snapper before me had lasted only three hours. At morning break, which was announced with a jangle of a bell, this new worker had gone to the bathroom and had never emerged. After a while, someone had finally checked; the high window was wide open, and the snapper-to-be had apparently crawled out through the little square opening and flopped to the ground in the parking lot outside, flapping her wings with relief, taking off into the morning air. Jane said she hoped I'd stay longer.

I liked and admired her very much; she was stuck deep inside a sleeping bag factory, seeking and finding there some degree of self-respect. She was a steady worker, and she swam with the flow. But I didn't last long at all. I think my fictitious fiancé was a mathematician. I discovered Boone's Farm Apple Wine, gained weight, not self-respect, and gradually sank. I won't say I snapped. I don't remember if I quit or if they simply fired me for absenteeism.

I passed through other odd jobs; all my jobs were odd. I was a swamper, working on a sewer line in a new ski resort. I lived in a tiny log cabin built a century before in a mountain pass by someone with great resourcefulness, and my roommates were a boy who read Hesse incessantly and loved someone else, and a very large rat called a trade rat. The rat would eat up all our food and leave something in its place: we'd find the old socks he'd scarfed up on a previous foray in the empty soup pot, or a little pile of old rusty nails on top of the bread box where three muffins had sat the night before.

My job was to put enormous calipers on the heavy twenty-foot cast-iron water pipes. The project was badly managed, and by the time things got started, winter had set in. Each new section of ditch had to be dynamited out through the ever deeper frost line. It was extremely cold. I had to place the calipers at the exact middle of the pipe so that the backhoe with its side boom could lift it free, swing it level through the air, and lower it slowly into the ditch below, where workmen waited to fit it into the end of the last one laid. If I attached the caliper off center, or if I neglected to thoroughly scrape the ice and snow off, the long and heavy pipe would slip and drag, or leer about, wreaking havoc, dangerously out of control in midair. I held people's lives in my cold hands.

I was reading Carlos Castañeda at this time. Don Juan asks, "Does this path have a heart?" I didn't think so.

I returned to Cambridge and took refuge in a safe and ordinary library job, shelving and reshelving old unread books. My co-worker told me that the librarian hired me because he thought I looked like I wouldn't mind getting dusty. More jobs followed: lab assistant, dishwasher. I went to South America and taught English for a year—this part always impresses people if I put it on my résumé. Then back to Cambridge and more library jobs that my heart was never into. For a few years, I supplemented my income playing the piano, accompanying voice lessons and student recitals; this was sometimes wonderful work, and also looks interesting on a résumé, but I was not a good enough pianist to make a real living at it.

In recent years I've had better, steadier positions overall, in places I've liked: disorderly, left-wing, nonprofit, well intentioned. But identifying with the general background is not at all the same as doing the job well, and I have a short attention span for many details. I don't feel I am climbing any noncorporate ladder or developing any particular career, and when the time comes to update my résumé, it is a difficult task.

I generally leave out the snapper and the swamper. Grimly I sort through the rest of my employment history. If I word it just right, I can sometimes invent a whole new, employable being, a vibrant, detail-oriented individual possessing exemplary organizational skills, long and varied library and office experience, and strong outside interests. This done, I take my uneasy mind off content and busy myself with format. I fix each paragraph with little bullets or asterisks or perhaps leave them with the elegant simplicity of neither. I design the layout with indents and tabs and tasteful spacing, and I set off the main sections of employment and education with smart italics, brave bold print, or the understated modesty of plain lettering. Sometimes I include a separate section: "Other Skills." It can be very depressing.

When I knew I was really moving, I applied to everything and anything within a radius of fifty miles from my cabin that did not require higher degrees in law or social work or education. I knew I would be lucky to get any job in Vermont, the way the economy was going, and I was. I was hired as a secretary in a good, serious, well-intentioned organization, well to the left of center at any time you might want to measure. There were struggles ahead; I felt defensive, and guilty too, when my new employers gradually realized what I was, and what I was not. I wanted to apologize when they inevitably discovered my lack of organization; I hadn't meant to mislead them. I tried hard to make up for it, for myself, whatever. It was a good job, and I wanted to keep it so. My attitude was certainly improving, even if my skills had not.

EXTERIORS

THE CREW HAD left the outside of the addition well wrapped in Tyvek, a durable, permeable, waterproof paper that you mount on the plywood sheathing. I felt no particular rush, and siding was a major decision to make. I took my time to make it rationally and studied house exteriors wherever I went.

Most of the older houses are simple capes with clapboard siding, which looks very nice. I found out it comes in long pieces; you nail them up with each row overlapping the one below. I learned that there are several different kinds of wood to choose from, each requiring a different finish, stain, or paint. The cabin's exterior was board-and-batten, which is a pattern of wide vertical boards with narrow strips covering each seam. Logically, I could put more of this on the addition to match. This type of siding is simple and inexpensive, but rustic and rather drafty. Vinyl siding was efficient, but unacceptably unnatural. Shingles were familiar to me and reminded me of Long Island, where I'd spent summers as a child, but they required the most work to put up and are not that common in Vermont.

I wasn't sure how to choose. Then one day I was at a building supply store to get a new hammer; there, stacked up outside the door, were bundles of pine shingles, on special for the month. The bundles cost eleven dollars each. They beckoned. They would fit in my car, which is an attribute that no other kind of siding had. This, then, was the deciding factor. Two bundles fit in the back, and two, on the backseat.

My building books applauded my choice: shingles are beautiful and enduring. One book, however, also drily noted that the shingler might find the pace of work a bit "glacial." It's true, it takes forever; I am still shingling my house and may still be for years to come.

It proved to be easy enough work once I learned how, although many, many shingles are required to cover any space at all. Around the windows and along the edge of the slanted roof, the shingles need to be cut at just the right length or angle, and there are many windows. Cutting them is painstaking work and involves climbing up and down ladders all the time with measuring tape and saws and utility knives. Since it is outside work, it can only be done in good weather, when it is tempting to do other things. The pace may also be further slowed by the fact that I enjoy it. Julian helped a lot during the early stages, but in latter years I have claimed the project as my own.

The first shingles I bought, the bargain brand, turned out to be full of knots, and many of them were ragged and very rough. In the early days, after hours of working in the hot summer sun, I started chanting deliriously to these shingles. "Fuzzy Wuzzy was a shingle," I sang, and then switched to the higher grade of smooth and knot-free shingles that cost eighteen dollars and up per bundle. The overall cost is spread over so many years that it doesn't really matter that it's not a bargain anymore.

From long experience, I've learned to shingle only when the fancy strikes. I carry my carefully selected, precut shingles under one arm when I climb my ladder, and then I balance them carefully on the top rung against the house. If it's too windy, my shingles blow down before I have had a chance to nail them securely to the wall. If it's too hot, I worry that I'll get sweaty and slippery and lose my grip and fall; if it's too cold, I'm afraid that my fingers will go numb and I'll drop the hammer on Lily. Fear of heights takes many forms. On the other hand, if it's just the right time of year, just the right time of day, and I'm in just the right mood, it's a fine way to spend an afternoon. Some of my rows may come out less than perfectly straight, less than perfectly consistent with the row below or above, but I don't care. It's my handiwork, and if I spend a lot of time standing back and admiring it, marveling at the crisp, varied shades of light and knotless pine, it only makes the pleasure last a little longer.

This is how it's done: I climb up on a ladder, high up in the air, leaning all my weight against the wall for security. I use a long board as a guide for the rows; I hold it horizontally against the wall, trying to keep it level as I tack it on. With one hand I prop the shingles up on this board, one after another, and with the other hand I nail them in place. At the end of each row, I perch precariously at the wall's edge and hope that one wall's rows will match the next. All this close contact—leaning, holding, knocking, and hammering on my walls—gives me a sense of the size, the feel, the very sound of my addition that I wouldn't get from anywhere inside. I can reach around the corners of the outside walls and hold its whole huge structure in my outstretched arms, pat it gently with my hands. I drum on it with my fingers. This is my outside, my protection from the cold and wind and snow and rain. High up on my ladder, I lean my body against it to keep from falling. There is a sunny, cool breeze on my bare arm, and I hold on to my house for dear life.

ANTENNAS

FALL COMES EARLY to Vermont, and with it, the prospect of prolonged cabin fever. Many people use television as an antidote. I have two, an old black and white that I keep stored under the stairs, and a newer one with color and remote control, which I use only for videos. I get only one station, and that hardly at all; this does not dismay me particularly since I never have watched television regularly. Anyway, you can rent videos at the gas station and the country store, and I don't mind driving far away to find a video store with more selections.

But the lack of TV reception does bother Julian. He likes television and is used to watching it. It is his observation post. He reports to me the thickening plots of weekly shows, keeps me up-to-date on the local Boston news, describes to me the slow maneuverings of our forgotten astronauts, or the current stalemates of the city council, or the intricacies of total hip replacement operations. He watches channels far and wide, and I certainly see the appeal. Still, for me, the bad, the boring, the inane, the noisy, the irresponsible, and the overslick of television outweigh the good. Julian likes to channel-surf, which I do not. When he doesn't like something he just flips to another station, and for him, the good prevails.

He kept his TV impulses in check until after the first addition was built. This addition gave the house a new height and, with that height, new reception possibilities. Just down this road, after all, just past one curve, my neighbor gets three or four stations easily and clearly, with the aid of only one elementary antenna. Our addition lifted the roofline and therefore the potential antenna location up another ten feet. Maybe that was all that was needed.

Julian's first antenna here was homemade. It was his cabin fever project, and he set to it with high and happy hopes, after feverishly consulting all the books on antennas in the local library. Oddly enough, there were several. His antenna was deceptively simple, two three-foot lengths of copper tubing positioned end to end, with a small separation between them. I have absolutely no idea why it should work. It is an indoor antenna, still bolted securely to the upstairs ceiling, and it did seem to make some difference to the clarity of our one TV signal, though it failed to bring in any others.

Undaunted, he began researching and eventually bought a premanufactured antenna. Or rather two. The first he bought resembled an actual insect's antenna under high magnification, long and thin with feathery branchings. Julian hooked it up to the television and then climbed out on the roof, twirling the antenna slowly while rotating it through all the points of the compass. I watched the varying intensities of static on the TV screen and shouted my reports out the window and up to him. "I think I see someone's head!" I remember calling, and that, I believe, was the extent of our Public Broadcasting Service reception. Failure was a disappointment. I felt it too.

The next antenna looked something like a grid, simple and structurally sound. He found it in a local hardware store and figured that since it was what the locals used, it must work. But it didn't.

Sometimes he still talks about getting a higher pole to mount our growing thicket of antennas on, but he is not as optimistic as he used to be. From time to time, we discuss getting a satellite dish. I am relieved, Julian regretful, that the installation and monthly fees are so high. But dishes and their fees are getting smaller and smaller, and I wonder if we will inevitably have one if we stay here long enough. Already they stud the Vermont countryside, as common as cows. The older and larger models stand in the corners of yards or hide modestly behind bushes on the edges of hillsides; the newer, more discreet versions perch on tops of roofs, alert, poised, ready to catch that magical signal transmitted from anywhere on earth, reflected off some unseen satellite, bounced from starry sky to TV screens across the land: CNN, or Home Shopping, or New England Sports Network, or any of the other eighty-three channels available in the most basic installation package. It is our world; we've made it so.

For the time being, we have moved our TV and VCR down to the first floor, detaching them from the whole antenna complex. We can always set up my old black-and-white TV with its rabbit ears at the times when it seems unbearable not to join in and watch the world's latest news disaster. But for the most part, we have given up on TV altogether and watch only videos. This is fine with me. I look forward to buying some kind of TV cart so that I can wheel it away in disgrace between viewings to some hiding place beneath the stairs. For me the television looms too much over the living room, fixing us in its blank and uncompromising stare.

Meanwhile, however, much has changed, as Amelia runs into the living room. The television has already grabbed her wandering attention. She is eighteen months old and will clamor endlessly for a book, then snap it shut after two or three pages; the remote controls, however, will mesmerize her for minutes on end as she turns the televised snow-show on and off. I swear I won't let TV be her babysitter, but at times, with very mixed and somewhat desperate feelings, I find myself encouraging her to watch. I've rented children's videos, and Julian brings us tapes of *Sesame Street*. We have a copy of *Casablanca*; I'll put it on and let it run its course for her. She'll watch anything for a while, though I'm not sure what she sees.

She is fascinated by shadows and reflections. When we walk down the road she sometimes likes to walk in my shadow, wherever it falls, her hand's shadow holding mine. The sun is low in the sky in fall and winter, and I sometimes have to chase after her as she follows her own shadow in a long diagonal across the road. She seeks out reflections in mirrors, spoons, plates, windows, and our TV screen, whose convex face catches the room as clearly as the wide-angle lens of a camera. She will sit in front of it in the pint-sized armchair I bought her, put her feet up on my grandmother's little footstool, turn to pat the cushion of the sofa behind her, and order "Up!" (meaning "down"), and Julian and I will sit behind her. She will settle herself in with her blanket and her bottle and her stuffed puppy, as if for a long, long movie, and then she will find our reflections, and we will find hers, and we will all wave into the dark screen of the television and at one another.

It's her world, too.

WATER, PART TWO

THE NEXT WINTER arrived, of course. I hoped the foundation would solve the problem of my frozen pipes, since at least the pipes under the cabin would no longer freeze. But the problem was really out on the hill. Somewhere the line was buried too close to the surface, going over a shallow bit of ledge, perhaps. No one knew exactly what path the line took. If the conditions were right, as they often were, the line would freeze, and that would be that.

The basement did, however, give Julian room for creativity. He had bought an old pressure tank and pump for a few dollars at a yard sale, insisting, when I looked skeptical, that it would come in handy. We just needed a large container, he said. So midwinter, as soon as the line froze, off we went to the nearest farm supply store. We'd noticed the large stock tanks, the big vats that farmers put out for their cows' water and feed in the summer months.

I remember I was wearing a floppy hat, a long skirt, and the nice warm town boots I'd just bought. In the side yard, buried under two feet of snow, I found the biggest stock tank I'd ever seen, not that I'd seen very many close up. When I brushed if off, it was like a gigantic black plastic bathtub with a drain out the side. "Is this for sale?" I asked the salesman, beginning to feel a little idiotic. "Do you deliver?" is what I found myself asking next, as if it were a very large order of groceries and I were a queen. I don't know what came over me. I felt so out of place, and Julian was suddenly nowhere to be seen. I wanted to explain everything to this stranger, tell him the whole history of the water and the frozen pipes, show him that I wasn't just an eccentric flatlander, but I didn't know how to begin. Anyway, the salesman just said no, they couldn't deliver today, and yes, the tub was for sale, and he didn't seem to want to know anything more.

Burning with ridiculous embarrassment, we crammed the stock tank into Julian's truck and brought it home. We slid it down the stairs into the basement, where Julian rigged it up as a reservoir, hooked up the old pump and the pressure tank, and piped it all into the plumbing system. It was a glorious achievement, and it worked very well. If the days were warm enough, we would siphon water from the well up the hill to the stock tank in the basement with a long series of hoses and thus have real running water for two or three weeks of frugal use.

In any case, it turned out that many Vermonters had this problem, and people were kind and sympathetic. It made me feel less an outsider, having my line frozen. People at work offered me showers during the winter and brought me bottles of drinking water from their homes. I barely had to mention it. The veterinarian said I could use the sink there anytime to give Lily a bath. In many ways it made me proud, surviving this hardship. Pride made it easier.

A STEP TOWARD AMELIA

IT WAS A year or more after I had moved up. There were still many more preparations to make before I could think of bringing a child home, but I was learning how to live and deal with the major problems that presented themselves, and this in itself was progress. I still liked my new job, and I still had it, and Julian and I were together and doing well. And we'd done a good job on the house; in return, it had brought out the best in us. It was hard to avoid a sense of accomplishment.

I loved my funny-looking house and I knew that Julian did too; just the thought of it could cheer me up. I had wound up with this odd addition, bigger than a bread box, one and a half stories high and halfway to my dream tower, stacked at the back of the long, low cabin like the ankle of a boot. I felt rather like the little old lady who lived in a shoe, only, of course, I had no children yet. I had no excuse not to reopen my adoption applications; I was forty-four, it was now or never, and I couldn't choose never. Now seemed impossible too, but in order to keep my options open I needed to update my paperwork.

The basic personal report, called a home study, is valid only for one year. Much had changed since I'd had mine done in Massachusetts, and I was afraid I would no longer be eligible to adopt a child. I was ready to defend my modest means and smallish house and ever advancing age, but the agency I'd called just agreed that I should adopt a child sooner rather than later. They said I would still be eligible for several programs; China, for instance, welcomed older parents.

The social worker I talked to told me not to worry about my small house or my salary. "People fret about the strangest things," she said kindly. Only the other day, she told me, a couple had called wanting to know if having running water was a requirement for a successful application. Carefully, I asked her what she had told them. I was having some problems myself, I said. In fact, I added ever so casually, I might have asked the very same question.

I didn't tell her that running water was the least of my anxieties, but she may have known that already. She'd been in the adoption field a long while.

I worried about everything. Who wouldn't? I feared that I was indeed too old, too set in my ways. I worried about Lily and how she would take to sharing my company; I did not want to hurt her. I worried I would have no solitude and go crazy. It was my decision, but obviously it would affect Julian too; clearly it would change our life together. He seemed positive and open and curious, but I knew he was ambivalent and scared as well. Who wouldn't be?

I had many questions. How could we possibly know how it would all turn out? What if it were a disaster? What if my child were somehow the wrong child? What if I couldn't love her? What if she couldn't love me? What if she were allergic to dogs? I didn't know that many babies, and it had been ages since my nieces and nephew had grown up. How could I take care of one myself? How could I possibly take this step with so many fears and so many questions?

Hope was also there, though, singing away in the backseat, balancing out fear just enough. And so I went ahead, and soon my basic paperwork was valid for another year. I'd taken a step toward Amelia.

THE ROAD

MOST OF MY immediate family lives in or around New York City. It is a long drive to central Vermont, and there is no easy way around it. My father died two years after I moved to Vermont; he had been very ill for five or six years, too ill to travel. So he never did see my cabin or its transformations, and he never met my daughter. Amelia didn't arrive until after he died.

I tried to visit New York as often as I could during his long illness. Because my parents couldn't travel to Vermont, I would bring them photographs of the house, in all its rural splendor. I shot rolls and rolls of film, taking detailed explanatory pictures of every inch of the place, from inches away: artistic close-ups of molehills and snowdrifts, drops of water and piles of leaves, of my first lettuce plants, the early crocuses, the first apple blossoms, the rose petals. I took countless pictures of Lily framed by the different locations: under the apple tree, on the porch, in the shade of the willow tree, through the tall grass, around the small pond in the neighboring field. I chronicled each step of the progress on the house, and I would bring down more pictures of walls and shingles and drywall and insulation than anyone could possibly have the patience to sift through. I'd bear these pictures to my parents like presents, like offerings, hoping and trying to share something of my new life with my father while he lived. Tentatively, I told them of my tentative steps toward adoption. I told myself that these efforts mattered, and I know they did. But I also knew that no matter how often I could visit, it was still just visiting, not the same as returning home. I'd moved to Vermont, not New York City. I felt far away, and I was. I was always sad after these visits.

One weekend late in the summer before my father died, my parents had to leave their apartment for a weekend while windows were washed and carpets cleaned. They stayed in a hotel for a few days. My father was tired and disoriented, and he wasn't sure where he had woken up or what had happened in between. When I called him that weekend, the conversation was confusing at first. Slowly I realized that he thought he'd just come back from visiting me in Vermont, the visit that he'd never made. I'd grown used to his new voice, thin and tired and old, but graceful and exceptionally kind. He was telling me how glad he was to have seen my house. "And the road!" he exclaimed with wonder and real surprise, "the road is so beautiful!"

I was completely happy in that moment. Together we looked down whatever road we saw. Maybe it was the same one.

The roads in Vermont wind through valleys and around hills; the sides of the hills rise steeply to their flat tops. In some places the hills sit in mounds, sometimes looking rather like thimbles. Glacial scouring and the more recent history of grazing have helped to give the land its well-worn, sometimes worn-out shape, even in the annual riot of new growth. The grass is lush in summer, the fields a sea of ever changing green hues, rippling with the wind. My father might have imagined that from afar the forest cover lies like a blanket of thick moss over ancient, rounded stone. The whole midsummer countryside is green, and old, and very lovely indeed.

In the fall, at just the right light of early evening, the bare trees on hillsides stand out as distinct, dark shadows against a deepening western sky. There are places on the highway where the distance is just close enough to distinguish individual trees, even the smaller branches, but still far enough away to view the forest as a whole. Because there are no leaves, you can see right through the trees to the bare ground they stand on. Along the hilltops and ridges the trees look like an even line of bristle, a row of cilia, a few days' stubble. They outline and emphasize the shape of the bare hills, form a fine and delicate border between old earth and the ageless sky. I think my father might have liked this.

Off the highway on the way to my house, the road follows smaller and smaller branches of rivers, up through narrower and narrower valleys, to finally reach the dirt road that goes along the stream to my cabin. On one side of this dirt road the land falls sharply to the stream below; on the other it drops to a shallow ditch, then rises again to a small open field and up to the hill beyond. In spring and summer the road is lined with wildflowers: asters and daisies and dandelions and Queen Anne's lace in a mix of dusty, wonderful smells. In late summer there are blackberries, too. There are all the signs of animal life and death: deer and raccoon tracks, snakes and frogs flattened by passing cars, enormous holes drilled out of dead trees by the elusive pileated woodpecker, the miscellaneous calls and chirps of other birds I'll never identify. One area is always cooler in the shade of some maple and hemlock trees, and late to thaw in spring; just beyond it there is often an oddly warm wind from across the field.

The road continues on with a steep climb through dark woods, but I think it used to end right at my house. From the driveway heading back, it slopes gently down, straight with a few wiggles to the first big curve and the next houses. For some reason this quarter mile or so looks longer to me than it actually is, maybe just because it is the longest perspective available. Anyway, I always feel some illusion of distance, as if I were looking through a telephoto lens.

After years of walks with Lily, now joined by Amelia, I know every inch of this road by heart; I can mark the passage of time and seasons by its changing details. Standing at my mailbox, I look down the dirt road; it's my daily view. I look down at the earth, familiar and close at hand. I like to remember that here, too, my father might have found much beauty.

THE SECOND ADDITION

Room for Amelia

ONE MORNING

HERE COMES AMELIA again.

"DO YOU LET Amelia play with eggs?" a good friend inquires one morning, sounding just a little frayed on the other end of the phone eighty miles away. We used to play Beethoven violin sonatas together regularly. We haven't played for a very long time. I consider. "Cooked, or raw?" I ask. There is a short pause. "You see," I hear her saying to her own young daughter, "Amelia doesn't play with eggs either."

I think it is Tuesday. Families throughout New England are trapped inside by the large, floppy, very depressing flakes of snow that are falling everywhere. It is cold. I wish we lived in a warmer climate. I've taken time off work to stay at home with Amelia. This morning I wish I had a job to go to. Lily is stretched out in the exact middle of the kitchen floor; she has a way of lying down that is gravity itself. Amelia is bored and has been almost ceaselessly demanding apple juice; she pronounces it as one word, "applejuice," and so well that it is often impossible to resist her.

She is about a year and a half old and just started talking a few weeks ago. Most words are indications rather than pronouncements, a mere initial consonant with a rising or falling intonation. "Buh," or "Cah," for instance, can stand for any number of life's necessities: bottle, blanket, bear, book; cow, car, cookie, cracker. She says "applejuice," however, flawlessly and without hesitation, giving the three syllables equally careful weight: ah-pull-jewss, perfectly formed, like the unfurling petals of a beautiful rose, like the shining of a precious jewel. Like Amelia herself, in fact.

For a short while, it was her proud word for everything. "Applejuice!" she would cry, pointing to a duckling in one of her books. "Applejuice!" she would yell at a bicycle in another. On our many car trips to nowhere in particular, I would hear her calling excitedly and indiscriminately at cows, houses, trucks, trains: "Applejuice!" She now has a bottle of apple juice, her third, and a rice cracker, which she is trying to foist off on Lily, who doesn't like them either.

Later: We are still in the kitchen—it seems we are always in the kitchen, despite having built not one but two additions. I am trying to make lunch, stepping around Lily and around the contents of the cupboard, which are now strewn about on the floor. I pick out my saucepan to heat some water for noodles. Something is clanking inside: a wrench. I know Amelia stashed it there; I figure that Julian gave it to her. Last weekend I overheard him talking to her, teaching her new multisyllabic words. "Socket wrench, spark-plug wrench, Phillips-head screwdriver" he was saying patiently, holding each item up in turn, gently showing her how they worked. She was entranced. It is 11:53. I hand the wrench to my daughter.

There is still time before lunch to get in the casual and upbeat little lecture that I've been told to give about peeing in the toilet and how Amelia might like to pee or poop there too, maybe, someday. I brought home a potty for her a week or so ago. "Let her familiarize herself with it," the accompanying booklet suggests. "Encourage but do not push her." Today she listens to me solemnly for a moment and then throws back her head, laughing so hard she almost falls down as she backs her way out of the bathroom, holding the end of the unraveling roll of toilet paper. I hear the echo of my words and see myself, forty-seven years old, sitting on the toilet, snatching at the disappearing toilet paper, laughing hysterically over pee-pee with my very young daughter. I check in her little potty and find that wrench again, along with a wooden block, a dish towel, the latest electric bill, a cork, a mayonnaise jar lid, and a wooden number 7, which was part of an educational jigsaw puzzle whose other pieces are scattered elsewhere.

It is noon. We are all a few hours older, the house is a few hours messier, and we will soon have lunch. I wonder at what has happened to my life, as another morning slips by. Eventfully, uneventfully—I cannot say for sure.

A car pulls into the driveway. I know who it must be. A woman and her teenage son, both dressed in black, approach the house with deliberate little smiles on their faces and familiar little pamphlets in hand. I open the door to my second question of the day. "Have you ever thought about why people grow old and die?" the woman asks slowly, peering at me and Amelia intently with her awful smile, holding out her pamphlet with its flames of Judgment Day. Her son looks sullenly around the kitchen. For a long moment I stand paralyzed, can't find the answer that will make them go away. "My noodles are boiling over" is what I finally manage, and then they leave, driving off on their mission of hope and salvation to the next house down the road. Amelia, who has just learned how, waves bye-bye. We eat our lunch. Life continues.

RAISING THE WALL

TELLING MYSELF I could always back out again, I had found out more about adopting from China. It was a program that had just closed down for a while, but it promised to reopen soon and would work well for single women over forty. The fact that it was on hold would give me a bit more time to prepare, I thought. And so I took more steps, sent off the updated home study and the finally completed pile of adoption paperwork to a Boston agency specializing in international adoption. I told my job supervisor that I might be applying for maternity leave at some undetermined future date. One day I bought what I supposed was an infant-sized pair of blue overalls, actually an enormous size three. With a growing sense of unreality, Julian and I hunted through yard sales for baby items. We bought a Kanga-Rocka-Roo, a baby monitor, a toy chest. Julian brought up his old high chair, which his parents had kept for him. It was like playing house. It was hard to believe that it would really happen.

"We need more room for a possible child" was how I always cautiously put it. We barely had room for ourselves, after all. And so Julian and I started work on our second addition, now leaning sturdily off the back of the first.

The total square footage available was limited by the location of the old septic tank in the backyard, by the shape of the land, and by the cost of lumber. The most we could fit within these confining factors was an area fourteen feet by thirty-two. We spent a very long time drawing plans on sheets of graph paper, measuring out little blocks, drawing lines, trying to visualize little square feet. We paced back and forth in the backyard and tried to imagine how the lawn would seem if it were a floor, how the sky would look if there were a roof, where the sun would fall, and we shuttered our eyes and pretended to look through windows in walls. At different times of day we would climb up the hill to look down on the empty backyard, trying to imagine it filled in by house.

Interiors, exteriors—we had our separate obsessions as surely as if they were sex-determined, which maybe they were. I saw inner dimensions, figured layouts. I envisioned a music room in which I would really practice again, working my way through Bach partitas with the steep green hill-side out the window. With much apprehension, I envi-sioned my possible child in a child-sized room. We needed closets. We had a bathtub currently on its side outdoors, near the garden in the front yard. It really should be indoors. But once again, I'd planned too small an addition. How could a space fourteen feet by thirty-two possibly accommodate a piano, a child, a bath, a closet, and a con-necting hallway? It was a topological puzzle without a real solution.

Julian mostly left it to me. His passion was studying how to actually build, how to attach and join the exterior walls, how to figure the slant of the roof and what space to allow for adequate venting and insulation—in essence, how to secure the exoskeleton of the whole thing, without which, I had to admit, there would be no interior anything. He learned, then taught me, about king and jack studs, cripples, headers, rafters, beams. Then he calculated the amounts of lumber and nails and set up a work plan.

The foundation was poured and the deck laid, and we started out one hot summer day with the high freestanding wall that would contain the beautiful old window, seven feet high and eight feet wide, that I'd found to go in my piano studio. I thought this would be the easiest wall, since so much of it was to be window and thus just open space within an outline. But it turns out that a window is actually an archway. Since there are no vertical studs in the window to bear the weight of the roof above, the board that spans the space above the window, called the header, must be extra strong and thick. The wider the window, the more substantial it should be. Julian nailed several wide, long boards together to make a heavy and indestructible beam for our header.

I hadn't realized that you actually build a wall horizontally, laying it out flat on the ground and nailing it together. Then you lift it up at what will be the top, get underneath to hold it over your head, and just walk toward what will be the bottom, going hand over hand and tilting it up and away from you. Supposedly it rises as surely as the sun or moon rises until it reaches its own perfect, vertical balance under the sky. We nailed our wall together, stood at either end of what would be its top, and started to lift. Somehow we got it enough off the ground to get under it, in position to start walking it up.

This was the point at which I discovered what was for me a brand-new and very urgent phobia: the Fear of Heavy Objects. Lying on its side, the wall looked light and vaulting, but it was twelve feet tall and had that header built in. Off the ground, it felt like it weighed a ton, and there I was, barely holding it up over my head, all the muscles in my body beginning to give out. There was no way I was going to walk anywhere. I honestly thought I was going to be crushed beneath its terrible weight and subsequently so would Julian. He was doing fine holding up his half of the wall but he would not be able to hold up the whole thing. No one would. It would be a ridiculous and tragic end for the two of us, crushed by our very first wall, and I could see it coming.

I conveyed my terror to Julian, and we somehow got out from underneath; and what a relief it was. We sat down shakily on our heavy, horizontal wall and wondered what to do with it. We were too proud or too embarrassed to ask any of the very nice neighbors down the road for help. It seemed important to do this ourselves, though I was skeptical about the whole operation. In many practical matters, I am the pessimist, the one of the two of us who insists that the grass will never grow, the water will never thaw, the car will never start, the snow will never melt, the whatever will never whatever. I thought we would never succeed, no matter how much help we got. Julian is the one with more faith, along with an innate practical ingenuity. Grass will grow, he promises, and it does. Water thaws, he claims, and he is usually right. He almost always gets the car going. We would get this thing up, he said.

It was a lesson to learn. Julian removed the header from within the framed wall with his super saw, which saws through anything and everything, and we did manage to walk the wall up; it was mostly just empty space for the window, after all. Then we each took an end of that extremely heavy beam, climbed high up on our separate stepladders, I balancing my end on top of my head, and somehow managed to slide it into place, all five hundred pounds of it. I exaggerate, but I would like to impress an audience, any audience, with how risky the operation was. It could have been a disaster. Instead, it was our first rock-solid wall, our first big window. When it was nailed in place, we could hang by our hands from that header and swing back and forth, pretending to look out and in.

After this, the remaining walls were child's play, relatively speaking, although the roof presented many of its own challenges. We finished the exterior framing within a week or so. When it was just its framed skeleton, no plywood sheathing over the studs, it was particularly beautiful, inside and out. By sunlight it was our proud and gleaming Parthenon, by moonlight our shadowy bare-boned ship, ready to float free across the backyard, over the septic system, set sail off the back hill and down to the stream below. Anything was possible.

WATER, PART THREE

WITH ALL THE ongoing winter problems of frozen lines and pipes, it had never occurred to me to worry about the quality of the water. I was just happy if I had it. This all changed one day, however, when Julian and I came upon a very dead cow lying near the brook in what appeared to be a farm animal dumping ground, a mile or so upstream from my cabin. Then of course I worried unhappily about lots of things in the water, and this concern was pretty overwhelming. I got some sampling kits from the local water-testing lab and took down a scientifically sampled bottle of my springwater.

The result was "coliform too numerous to count." This was not a very nice phrase, but I wasn't sure what it meant. Did it mean that the technician really sat and tried to count, really fast, one two threefourfivesix, eleventwelve thirteennineteen twenty . . . thirty-seven, no, thirty-eight?

Or did it indicate a swarming mass of millions and millions of coliform? Whatever were they, anyway? The lab had a standard response: boil the water for twenty minutes and periodically flush the whole sorry system out with Clorox. Other people said I would have gotten sick already if the water was bad. Coliform were not necessarily bad, just sometimes bad. It was very confusing. I tried to believe what I wanted to believe, but I wasn't even sure what that was. I started buying bottled water. "Pure Vermont Spring Water," proclaimed most of the brands I bought.

After we had framed in the second addition, I hired someone to do some necessary leveling of the ground around the back of the foundation so that we wouldn't turn into a swamp. This man said he could also fix the well. His theory was that the contamination had been caused by all the hay I'd piled up on top of the well over the years to keep it from freezing. He said that he could dig it out and clean it up and dig a deeper trench and put in a real concrete-tiled well, if that was what I wanted. I went up the hill and checked inside the well. There was a dead mouse floating there.

So I told him to do it all, dig it out, dig a trench, put in a clean concrete well with a real cover. Surely that was what I wanted. It had been a damp summer, and the ground was boggy. My man went up the hill in his gigantic bulldozer, rolling up the grass in the deep treads like a thick carpet, and then he slid back down on the newly created mud slide. I couldn't bear to watch this and left for work. When I came home at the end of the day I had a new well, towering high up above a hill of devastation.

Meanwhile, my office mate at work was having problems with her well water. We would start out each day telling each other how very not well we felt, but oh well, all's well that ends well, we would just get the job well done, only we didn't feel so well off, and so on. Her problem cost her thousands of dollars; she had to have her well redrilled. For a short period of time, I felt lucky, or sort of lucky. My new well and line had not cost thousands. My grass and garden would recover, maybe, someday.

As it turned out, however, I really should have left well enough alone, for within a few weeks things began to deteriorate, or rather, began to smell as if they were deteriorating. The water turned grayish brown and developed an odor like rotten eggs. It got so I couldn't even turn the faucets on, the stench was so bad. It was a nightmare. I got out one of my old sampling kits from the local water-testing lab and took them my little sterile jar full of putrid water. "What do you think this is?" I asked them, pointing to the strands of gray matter floating in the murky liquid, opening the jar for them to smell. "That's disgusting," they answered simply. And that was the test result, the one free ride in the whole saga.

So I had a well drilled. Not immediately, but soon. It cost thousands of dollars and the water is rock hard, but it is clear, cold, completely odorless, and runs all year round. It has only insignificant traces of coliform. It is suitable for human consumption, even by infants, and just in time, too. It is, I must say, well worth it.

But it is still curious to me how easy it is to readjust and take running water completely for granted again. We thought we would miss the challenge, necessity being the mother of invention and all. But the stock tank lies on its side in the backyard now for strangers to puzzle over, and I feel no pangs of regret. The hillside has finally grown over again, and that new concrete-tiled well looms a bit less prominently, less like the folly it truly was. The whole consuming problem has just vanished, like I'd never had it.

HEAT, PART TWO

JULIAN BROUGHT UP a weather monitor, a gadget that measures temperature and barometric pressure and wind speed and rainfall and stores all this information indelibly in its tiny electronic brain. You press one of its little buttons and it gives an answering chirp, and there, in the display, is our present environment, inside and out. Another button and another little chirp and the monitor recalls the environmental extremes within whatever span we ask it to. So anytime we wanted to, we could look up the coldest, direst, dampest, windiest, most miserable time of any day or night we chose. Our Vermont-style antenna now had a miniature windmill whirling around it, and the outside temperature gauge and rain collector draped out the back window. We kept in close touch with the elements.

I may have scoffed, and I probably did, but it was somehow gratifying to know that the indoor nightly temperature of the addition often hovered in the forties, sometimes falling well into the thirties. "No wonder I felt cold," I could tell myself in the morning. It was the kind of information I would often casually let drop. I hoped Vermonters would think me hardy, if a fool.

Anyway, I'd grown used to sleeping in the cold; I'd even grown to prefer it. In winter, we moved the comfortable chairs to the kitchen and sat around the space heater there for warmth during waking hours. When I wanted to practice, I'd set up two electric heaters aimed strategically at my piano stool. But obviously this was not a lasting solution, especially if there was to be a child. And for all my being accustomed to the cold, I was beginning to feel a little eccentric. It began to seem weird, difficult even, to take off my coat indoors in other people's houses. Whenever I met someone new I wondered only what clothes they wore to bed. Sometimes all I wanted to talk about was heat.

Julian was the plumber and the guide. He explained to me the differences between furnaces and boilers, between natural gas and oil, and we discussed the pros and cons of radiators, baseboard heat, wall units, direct vents. He showed me with diagrams how hot air, steam, water, and electric systems worked; we thought fleetingly of solar energy. I remembered houses from my childhood, remembered standing over the heating grates, my clothes puffing out and filling up with hot air, my blown-away hair hot and dry. It was a beautiful memory. Julian said hot air was the simplest to install, and he could easily do it alone. We began to collect beautiful old grates at yard sales and salvage places.

We had a chimney, but it only reached down as far as the first floor. It would be a major production extending it further down and through the foundation wall, so Julian decided we should get a direct-vent furnace that would blow whatever it blows out the side of the wall rather than up through a chimney. We shopped around. Julian told me just what to ask for on my own: propane gas, direct vent, around 80,000 to 100,000 Btu. I felt very impressed with myself, walking into a plumbing supply store by myself and spouting all these technical terms; I would half expect the salesmen to burst into a round of scattered applause after my initial inquiries. But they seemed less in awe than I that I would know so precisely what I wanted. They'd quote me a price, usually too high, and that would be that.

Julian finally found a good deal in the classifieds: two scarcely used furnaces for the price of one and a lot of extra ductwork to go with it. We didn't need two furnaces, but it was a deal not to pass up. As it turned out, only one of the two actually worked, but I'm not complaining. Good deal or not, it is warm now.

Amelia arrived later that same year, and we had plenty of time to get heat to her small room before the cold weather. I say we, but I mean Julian. He did it all. Because of him, the basement now has a network of elegant, square tunnels suspended from the ceiling, piping piping-hot air to almost every room. The direct vent shoots out the side, looking rather like a horizontal pipe of a church organ, set to hoot some low and rumbling note and send it echoing down the narrow valley.

The furnace does turn out to be uncommonly loud. After years of doing without heat, I like its noise; it is easily as fine as the sound of indoor plumbing. In the hush of wintertime, when I am taking Lily and Amelia for our walk down the road, I can hear it all the way from the next bend in the road. There is a huge exhaling sound, followed by a distant, shuddery mechanical roar. I find myself scanning the sky for airplanes, watching the road for trucks. But it is only our house, our lovely, warm house, blasting on the heat.

USED CARS

"WHY DON'T WE take a peek at the oil?" is Julian's tactful reminder that I haven't done so in thousands and thousands of miles. My friend knows and understands and loves anything with a combustion engine, and it is because of him that I have the oil changed regularly, but this is all I manage to do.

We've both always had old cars, or rather, a series of old cars. In the nine years we have known each other, we've had eight cars between the two of us. It is fortunate that we enjoy shopping for new used cars so much. We actually welcome the demise of a vehicle, in a bittersweet sort of way.

My car, an old hatchback with 150,000 miles on it, had begun to seem less than reliable. It had rusted badly above the windshield and somewhere through the hood, so that when it rained outside, it also rained in on my lap and on my feet, which I really hated. Finally, it smelled very strongly of wet dog, many years of wet dog in fact, which Julian really hated. It seemed time to look for another one.

Simultaneously, Julian's truck's engine was fizzling out. Ironically, it had something to do with oil. He needed a replacement soon.

"Volvo," we thought together, as great minds sometimes do. A family car, and here we were, on the verge of perhaps becoming a new family: it seemed the Responsible Thing to Do. It was a preparation we felt able to make. I traveled to Boston one weekend, and we planned to spend three days hunting through city and environs for the perfect and affordable family car.

Volvos, however, even old, used-up ones with hundreds of thousands of miles on them, are very expensive. It was hard to find one cheap enough to even consider looking at. The first ad we followed up led us directly to a junkyard, not a good sign at all. The old Volvo sat there, a bit apart from the yard itself; it was dark green and quite nice looking, but what bad luck, regretted the proprietor who had emerged from the shack of an office, its strut had collapsed, and so we would be unable to test-drive it today. Though, of course, he could vouch for its excellence and reliability. In the meantime, was there anything else he could offer us? He waved to the lot of junked vehicles. Were we interested in Volvos particularly? If so, he had gotten in another just this past hour. Gentleman had brought it in. He pointed to a very battered old station wagon with crushed fenders and a door handle that hung limply from its socket. Eight hundred dollars and it was ours, he would fix it up as good as new. Cosmetics, that's all it needed. They don't make them like that anymore, he said with a stern shake of his finger. His son-in-law already had his eye on it, but hey, he liked our looks, he'd let us have it for eight hundred.

He left us to our thoughts, and some other man—the son-in-law?—came out. "Sticker says eight hundred dollars, but you could probably have it for four," said this new salesman, lowering his voice along with the price conspiratorially and dramatically. He'd go to bat for us with the boss, maybe even get it down to three hundred. Say two-fifty. "Great deal!" he concluded, uttering his first real lie of the day. "The rubber alone is worth that much," he added, speaking his second.

I stayed in the lot, and Julian warily got in the driver's seat, started it up, and lunged out into the street in a billowing cloud of thick, acrid smoke. "You could skywrite with that thing," said our salesman, a touch of admiration in his voice. I waited anxiously in the junkyard. After a while, the salesman left and a young lad of nine or so emerged from the shack, carrying a strangely incomplete horn, which turned out to be half a saxophone. He demonstrated its solitary, shrill, bleating note, over and over and over. I began to feel just a bit tormented, as if I were lost in some futuristic or possibly Italian movie, surrounded by the wrecks and relics of our lost civilization, chased by an incessant pied piper. The boy stopped long enough to explain that his dad had got his instrument for him a week or so ago. "For free!" the heir to a junkyard said proudly.

We shifted our sights and searched instead for a truck for Julian. He came up with the idea of a truck with a plow, since this was snowy New England and we did have a driveway. And so we answered an ad for "Pickup with plow, little rust, runs very good, dependable cheap transportation." I forget what make.

It was way, way out of the way in New Hampshire, but it seemed like a good enough deal to take the trip. We followed a long dirt road to its very dead end, and there it was, next to a trailer and a bunch of sheds. The owner was out prying away at the hood with something long and sharp. Two empty beer cans rolled near the front tire, and a third balanced on the fender. The owner was a very frustrated man. Something about the starter motor had broken, something vital but insignificant, easily fixed, he said. But the hood had also snapped some vital linkage and was now closed permanently. He'd tried everything, he said bitterly, taking another swig. Maybe we should come back another day. Julian, however, is someone to whom all mechanical challenges are irresistible. He offered to help, and they went at it for hours with crowbars and screwdrivers and coat hangers, until Julian accepted his first beer and the owner finished his fifth. The starter motor remained trapped under the hood, and the truck probably still stands there, stock-still, stubborn, mouth clamped tight shut, like the little engine that couldn't, or wouldn't, or shouldn't.

We went on to many other possible good deals over the next two months: cars with stick-shift mechanisms that swung free between third and fourth gears, cars with alarming popping noises and ominous *thunks,* cars that simply died on the way out of the lot, cars with the spirit of half a saxophone.

I was the first to realize we were getting nowhere, building up our inventory of useless used cars. One day I finally just traded mine in for a newer model. Although I resented the price, was depressed by the color and the personalized season's greetings I received from the pushy salesman who forced a quick deal, I was glad I bought it. It had four fully functional doors, didn't leak, and would easily last another fifty thousand miles. I felt sensible and responsible behind the wheel of this newer vehicle. Shortly after, Julian bought the equivalent model of truck: newer than the old one, with a child-sized jump seat in the extra-large cab. And so we were set. At least we were ready for a child in the backseat of the car, even if her room was not yet fully framed in.

INTERIORS

I PACED THROUGH the open interior of our addition, raveling and unraveling my life within imaginary interior walls. Maybe my adoption plans would go through, but maybe they wouldn't; the program in China had already been shut down longer than I'd expected. I'd heard many stories of adoptions that had fallen through at the last minute; it was a notoriously unpredictable process. I was afraid that China would never reopen for international adoptions and I'd have to start the process all over again with a different program; I wasn't sure I could do that. And then, too, I was very afraid that I would back out again, run away again. I arranged and rearranged the future in endless configurations; it seemed both urgently necessary and quite impossible to be able to plan things out exactly. I thought the interior of this new addition would decide the future, setting it, if not in stone, at least in the rigidity of pine studs and sheets of drywall. And it would be good to have things finally settled, once and for all.

Whatever happened, I tried to tell myself reasonably, the corner where we'd thought to build her bedroom could just as well be a big bathroom, or a small studio for my piano, or a library. The big studio space I'd planned could be a spare bedroom, or a sunroom, or an extravagant panoramic space for the bathtub. The junk room we'd hoped for might turn out to be a small study for Julian. Or it too could be the bathroom, or another walk-in closet, or a tiny bedroom, or a meditation closet like I'd once seen in a Cambridge apartment. I would learn to meditate daily and become a true hermit. There were many possibilities, I told myself.

And so I tried to compromise with an unsure fate. The piano studio was tailored down to barely fit the piano or, possibly, a bed. The possible junk room we made big enough for a desk as well. Julian thought of a large corner cabinet he had in Cambridge; he'd been meaning to bring it up, and we made space for it wherever possible. The bathroom came out long and narrow, with just barely room enough for the bathtub, a tiny corner sink and a toilet. The space was equally suitable as a storeroom. We measured out the child's room just long enough for the piano; in case the child didn't arrive, it could be the studio. At the last minute, however, we remembered to include a closet. This shortened it two feet; the piano would no longer fit. I thought this was a fateful sign. I thought lots of things were fateful signs; I was looking for them everywhere as I waited for word of Amelia.

Then Julian wired in lots and lots of plugs to cover any future use for each room and ran telephone wire everywhere we could think of. As the resident expert in fiberglass, I spent a few weekends insulating as swiftly and painlessly as I possibly could. The child was somewhere in the future, possibly. The corner cabinet was, and still is, in Julian's Cambridge apartment. The piano's presence was indisputable, but nothing else was certain.

PAINTING THE FLOOR

PAINTING THE FLOOR of the studio was the last step before moving my piano to its new room. It had been a long time since we'd raised that first high wall, but the interior of the piano room was finally sheetrocked and taped and painted. The light switches worked. We laid the floor, wide boards of yellow pine, in a matter of days.

Then I decided to paint it. I'm not sure why, even. I chose some color from the color charts called Seafoam, or Sandpebble, or Soft Pewter, or Evening Dusk. Actually, it was just light gray, which was just what I wanted. The salesman said to get polyurethane paint for durability, so I did, along with a rather good brush.

Unexpectedly, it was pure bliss, sitting there on the bare wood floor in the beautiful new room we had built our-selves, the sunlight filtering through a late afternoon mist, bouncing off the shiny new paint and onto the off-white walls in shivery designs of reflected light. It felt so familiar; it took me a while to figure out why. When I did, I was back at my grandmother's house on Long Island, it was late summer, and I was sweeping the painted wood porch, the light mottling through the leaves of the enormous trees of the front yard and through the latticework of the porch, casting reflections and shadows on the side of the house. I was sure that I'd matched the exact color, even.

Of all the houses and apartments we lived in, my grandmother's house is the one I remember best; we went there almost every summer when I was growing up. And with my possible child's room at the other corner of the addition, I suppose I'd been thinking of my own childhood. Maybe the physical motion of painting had brought back the solitary late afternoons, solitude just this side of loneliness, the leaves that would catch in a whirlwind in the backdraft of the broom, then all get swept up and away in a big satisfying swoosh off the long, pretty porch. I thought I could catch the very smell of the late summer salt air. I missed the ocean, the beautiful, enormous, imponderable ocean. What was I doing so far inland? How had I ever landed here?

When I feel homesick, or what I think of as homesick, it is always a solitary emotion, a mix of happiness and sadness, discovery and loss, distant and familiar sensations.

Specific memories don't necessarily crowd in. It's just a passing moment, a glancing of time, a perception and sudden recognition of everything at once in one small instant. Then the cloud will move, the ray of sunlight will shift and hit some other spot on earth, and from where I stand, from where I stood, the world will seem ordinary again. But the moment catches and illuminates everything, and time stands still between one world and another, between afternoon and evening, between beginning and end. Sitting there on the floor of my studio with a brush and a bucket of paint, I thought I could see the world through the eyes of a child. I suddenly thought this place might feel like home.

I didn't lose my head and paint the entire house. I knew that the next day my floor might seem just gray. Life would go on, and in a few years I might well even move away, find someplace warmer and closer to the coastline. A while ago I might have asked, so then why paint the floor at all? Now, at age forty-eight, I'm only just beginning to figure this one out.

As I write this, my durable painted floor is beginning to show age and signs of wear. It's marred by scuffs and scrapes, scribbled on by Amelia. Dirt and leaves get tracked in regularly through the outside door of the studio, and dust piles up in the corners. I like this. It's an ordinary floor, no more and no less, something to sweep.

LADYBUGS

THOUGH WE MAY not see much wildlife, we do see lots of bugs. In spring and summer there are long lines of ants everywhere, and enormous crickets scatter with every step you take outside and jump out at you from empty cups and saucers indoors. In the summer evenings there are starry, ever changing constellations of fireflies in the orchard. Depending on the temperature and season, dense clusters of houseflies collect over the windows, while spiders scrabble desperately in the sink when you turn on the water.

One fall, hordes of ladybugs moved into my house. Not just mine, either—it wasn't because of my housekeeping or lack of it, I wasn't growing anything in my house that especially attracted them, I wasn't hanging out ladybug feeders. Many other Vermont houses were also infested (not my word) with thousands of these little beetles. The news reports and even the weathermen mentioned it.

While it wasn't unusual to have a few ladybugs indoors, no one could remember ever having quite so many. It was the end of a long summer; maybe the ladybugs were addled by the lingering hot weather, or maybe it was a new strain of beetles with new and different habits, or maybe it was some experimental collective decision that drew them indoors in such great numbers. It seemed like a sign of something, but no one knew exactly what. Anyway, the authorities advised us that these bugs were harmless, even beneficial, and said to simply scoop them up and put them outside if we wanted to get rid of them. Otherwise, they said, just let them be. They were just looking for a place to spend the winter.

When I first noticed them I assumed they were nails and screws that I'd imperfectly covered in my early attempts at drywall taping. Or maybe they were just random spots, I thought, little balls of dust and cobweb. Then I saw that they were all creeping slowly across the walls and windows and doors.

It was disconcerting at first, but when I realized what they were I loved watching them. I would find myself spending whole hours just staring at the walls. I'd sit in the newly painted studio and watch as two ladybugs started out their journeys from opposite corners of the room, scrawled their meandering paths across the vast expanse of off-white walls. They would meet somewhere roughly in the middle, bump into each other, back away a bit, and then straggle off again up to the ceiling corners. There the ladybugs formed clumps of themselves, pooling together like drops of water, piling up on one another for warmth or comfort or mating or protection or whatever reasons ladybugs clump. Julian and I had taken a course on insects a few years before; I looked up ladybugs in our entomology textbook. This clumping behavior still puzzles entomologists somewhat; they're not completely sure what it's for.

So my ladybugs were looking to begin their hibernation in the high corners of my rooms, holing up indoors for the long winter, and why not? My house has lots of weird angles, and in each angle, for a while, there was a collection of ladybugs. I read further in my insect books and learned that ladybugs seek the height of the horizon and often clump together on mountaintops. I liked thinking of my ceiling angles as their lofty peaks, as high as any small beetle could climb. I became very used to my housebound ladybugs and would wait patiently for any spot on wall or window to start slowly migrating, up toward the line of the hillside outside the windows and on to the highest reaches of my rooms.

That fall was a time when news of the human world was particularly depressing. In a climate of despair with strong currents of ill will, things seemed to be taking a turn for the worse. I'd heard, however, that ladybugs bring good fortune to those they alight upon, and I thought their arrival must be a good sign. I felt that my house was blessed by their presence while I waited for my future child. But I fretted over them too, wondered whether I should be turning up the humidifier, spraying them with fine mists, feeding them bits of aphids, shading them from the electric lights at night. My house, for all its inviting angles, was not their natural habitat, not their luckiest choice.

The Indian summer moved directly into an early winter, and it must have finally been too hot and dry for them with the furnace on. Maybe something had been badly unbalanced in their systems to begin with, global warming taking its early toll on small and delicate creatures, or perhaps I should have gathered them all into a paper bag as soon as they arrived and moved them to an outside shelter somewhere high up on my hillside. Anyway, I missed them when they were gone, for after a few months they mostly just dried out and died, one clump after another dropping off the wall in a shower of spotted wing flakes, catching in a cobweb, hanging by a thread, scattering like ashes, dust to dust.

WAITING

CHINA HAD CLOSED its adoption program so that the government could centralize and control the process. Whenever I called my agency for news, I always got the same answer: "It's only a temporary delay," they'd say. They had reliable information and good contacts. China would reopen soon.

In fact it was well over a year before China reopened to international adoption, and another six months before I got word of Amelia. During that time, I sought advice and information everywhere. "Difficulty at the beginning" was the memorable commentary the I-Ching gave me, but every month there were new rumors, new updates. For a while, I'd make huge efforts to find out all the latest news. It reminded me of when I first understood the meaning of the terms *luteal phase defect* and *anovulatory cycle* and thought it might make a difference just to know that there were such things. Similarly, I would seek out the monthly reports of governmental wranglings in China, read the speculations on which ministries were having power struggles with which others. There were rumors of changing regulations within the Immigration and Naturalization Service, and distant rumblings of a whole new set of rules proposed by the most recent International Conference on Adoption. For a while, I thought it helped to know.

I knew little about China. I'd taken a course in Mandarin twenty years ago just from curiosity; all I could remember were two phrases: "I gave my teacher a big black pencil" and "I often sing long songs." I checked out books in the local library and spent hours in the travel sections of bookstores. I tried to learn something of my future child's roots, but all I really cared to do was look at photographs of children, wondering whether I could love one or the other, worrying if I thought I could not.

It turned out that many prospective parents were caught "in the pipeline" of adoption, and it wasn't difficult to find people in the same situation I was in. "A roller coaster of emotions" is another stock phrase in the adoption world, and waiting families were all on the same long ride. There was a whole underground network of people waiting to adopt from China, and address and phone lists of families who had been through the process and who now had their children were available. Photos and even videotapes of previous trips were passed around like precious objects, signs of hope. I met someone in a nearby town who was also waiting for the program to reopen; we'd meet for lunch every few weeks, commiserate with each other, reassure each other, pore over photographs, obsess over the latest rumors. This did help.

The parents who had adopted children in years past were kind and encouraging. It began to seem entirely normal to me to call up total strangers, ask them personal questions about themselves and their children, confess my own very worst fears and doubts. Of course, I'd especially seek out parents who admitted to having been ambivalent and had overcome their doubts.

I tried to keep my glimmerings of hope alive, but often they would flicker out altogether. My father was very sick, slipping away. I hoped that he would meet my child—I wanted him at least to know that she was on her way—but he died that year long before China reopened to international adoption, long before Amelia was even born.

More time passed. My child seemed to grow only more distant. There were times when I no longer cared, and sometimes everything just seemed so sad.

In the spring, my family held a memorial service for my father. I spent many weeks preparing for it, helping to plan the music and the readings. Meanwhile, in a tangle of conflicting rumors, China was slowly reopening. My papers were sent to Beijing the week before my father's service. I could barely focus on my child; I saw her slipping away as well. In general I couldn't trust myself to feel one way for more than twelve hours at a time; my moods changed by day and night. Progress on her room stalled, ground to a halt, and life seemed permanently stuck on hold.

WHEN WORD FINALLY came, of course it seemed quite unexpected, almost out of the blue. My sister and brother-in-law had come to visit; we had just returned from a county fair. One minute Abby was explaining to me in some detail how she now felt about cows. The next minute the phone rang. It was some strange travel agent who called to tell me that I was to stop in Hong Kong overnight. He asked me if I wanted to sightsee for a day or two, or just fly on to China immediately. At first I didn't know what he was talking about.

The adoption agency had forgotten to call me first and had told this man to make the flight and hotel arrangements for prospective parents. All he could tell me was that I had a baby and a plane reservation the next week. So I learned that I was a mother-to-be, just like that, due in a couple of days. Julian and I just looked at each other for a moment of stunned silence, which I finally broke with a very strange, strained, yelping sound that I'd never made before: the sound of imminent motherhood. Smiling broadly, my wonderful sister cooked us dinner.

I was relieved to find that I had already decided to go. After years of agonizing, it came down to a simple yes or no. How could I say no?

I CALLED MY Boston agency. I found out that my baby girl was five months old and healthy. "What does she look like?" I asked the adoption worker who had yet to send me the photograph. "Well," she answered, after what seemed a very long silence. "She has a lot of hair." So off I went to China the next week, complete with one hundred little diapers, three tins of dry soy formula, three bottles, some incredibly small clothes I'd hastily bought, one toy elephant with a little red hat, a tiny dress with green and red flowers from my mother, a tiny purple jumpsuit with a picture of a popcorn bag from my sister Abby, a child-sized handmade quilt from my sister Judy, a massive last-minute panic attack, and the newly arrived photo from around the world—beautiful Amelia and her lovely thatch of hair.

DIFFICULTY AT THE BEGINNING

ONCE AGAIN, WE surveyed the bareness of an unfinished room. Light fixtures, drywall, paint, flooring, trim, were lacking. Ready or not, I went to get Amelia. Julian built her room. I was away three weeks. The trip was very hard; the I-Ching had answered accurately. Julian would reassure me with details of his progress when I called with my great distress.

By the time I waved good-bye to my old life, my panic attack had grown to pure and almost unbearable terror. I hurtled through space in an overcrowded jumbo jet to the other side of the world, off to bring back a total stranger who would dominate the rest of my life. I thought I could see with ghastly clarity what a disastrous venture the whole idea was. There were indeed excellent reasons not to have a child. I should have heeded them all. I must have been crazy. I should have just quit my job again if I'd needed so badly to change.

I was traveling with three other prospective parents. We were to be taken to the orphanage the night we arrived in order to meet and approve our new children before starting the paperwork in another city. Reeling with exhaustion after two full days of travel, we changed our sticky clothes, piled into tiny taxicabs, drove helter-skelter at breakneck speeds through ever increasing poverty, on roads that seemed less and less like roads, to the furthest outskirts of the city. It was too dark to see anything by the time we reached the orphanage. I couldn't believe that any of this was really happening.

It was the middle of the night, the middle of nowhere. The nursery was stark, two tables and a row of cots. The staff had handed me a small, pale, skinny, sad-eyed baby. We had an interpreter with us. This one is yours, they said.

She was so different from her photograph, I cried to Julian in my first phone call. They had shaved off all her hair except for a bit at the top. She was so thin and looked so strange to me. How could I love this stranger? Her head was flattened and wedge-shaped from lying in her crib so much. She was so distant; she never smiled. Julian told me he had taped xeroxed copies of her photograph to the refrigerator door and another on the door to her room so he'd see it many times every day. He had set up a work plan for the three weeks. The ceiling of her room followed the line of the shed-style roof. Where it was highest, he planned to build a shelf to store books and toys.

One week later, we returned to the orphanage for a second visit. Amelia looked at me and screamed. She hadn't been well, the orphanage staff said. They hovered about for a while and then brought out another baby. Healthier, they said. Take this one instead, she doesn't cry so much, they suggested with nods and smiles of encouragement. They had meant to be helpful.

It had made me feel so terrible, I told Julian from a world away. I didn't want to choose. I didn't want a different baby. I just wanted her to be all right. I just wanted *me* to be all right. I had felt so guilty to be glad to leave the orphanage that afternoon. From the other side of the earth Julian told me he had put in a dimmer so that the light wouldn't bother her eyes when we looked in on her at night. My nephew, expert at walls and drywall taping, had come up for a week to help out. Julian told me that they had made the closet from special, fancy plywood; it looked good, he said. He had already hung up the big blue overalls I'd bought.

It turned out Amelia was sick with gastroenteritis. She was in the hospital for a while, then she was out of the hospital, with me in one of the disconcertingly fancy tourism hotels that we were booked in. I had no experience with sick children. I had no idea how much to worry or not worry, so I worried about everything. She'd awakened crying five times the night before. I walked with her all night, up and down the anonymous halls. The plush hotel in a poor city on the coast of China had perpetual, canned classical Muzak in the halls and stairwells and elevators: the "Minute" Waltz, "Clair de lune," and Beethoven's Ninth Symphony, all processed to sound exactly the same. The world was insane. I hadn't slept for many days.

Parenthood was looking very hard to me. I was afraid I would ruin my life, her life, and Julian's as well, if he wasn't careful. Julian told me that he'd finished painting the walls a light, sandy color. He and my nephew were putting down her floor, the same wide pine boards we'd used in the piano studio. They planned to use this for the trim and windowsills as well; it made sense, it would bring the room together, he said.

Then, one day near the end of the trip, she stopped crying. This last hotel provided old-fashioned cribs with wooden beads strung through the slats. I heard an odd scrabbling sound one night; I looked over to my daughter to see her quiet and alert. She was reaching out with her long, thin fingers, kicking up with her skinny little feet, twirling the beads around and around, solemnly learning how to play, all by herself. I watched for a long time. It seemed like a miracle, but it was just her. Her life had changed even more than mine had, but she taught me to trust her, not the other way around. It made me cry, and the next morning she smiled.

And oh, what a smile. She was just right, beautiful, in an interesting, funky kind of way, with her shaved head and spiky tuft at the crown. She was calmer and eating all the time. Already she seemed stronger. When I told Julian this, I could hear his happiness. He said things were going very well. He had brought the comfortable rocker to her room; we could sit with her, watch over her while she napped. He had set up a shelf in the kitchen for her formula and bottles. He'd stocked the cabinets with rice cereal. Her crib was set up, all ready for her.

I made it through the rounds of paperwork. I found out that her Chinese name means "expectation," "anticipation," "hope." The room was on the north side of the house; we'd been concerned that it would seem dark and cold. Julian reassured me that her new room was shady but that it caught the first morning rays of sun through the trees.

"This may be hard for a while," I warned him from another lifetime, the sound of Amelia crying frantically in the background.

"That's all right," he said.

A ROOM FOR AMELIA

IT TOOK TWO days to travel back. Amelia had
diarrhea on the last flight; we were so tired that we sat on
the floor outside the occupied restroom and sobbed
together. My seatmate must have thought we were way out
of control. She spent the first half of the flight studying
lipstick advertisements, and the second half applying nail
polish. She didn't dare look our way. She didn't realize we
were just mother and daughter, getting acquainted.

The closer we got to the Boston airport, the better we
felt. We were almost at the end of our first long journey
together, almost at the beginning of another. A family was
met with crowds of relatives and flashes of cameras.
Amelia was plastered to me in her infant sling; we made
our way through the throng, blinking at the lights, and
found Julian waiting for us. Amelia gave him her heavenly
smile.

• • •

JULIAN WAS RIGHT; her room was lovely. I'd remembered only how small the bare space had seemed, but finished off it was airy and open and interesting with its high, slanted ceiling and built-in shelves. The yellow pine floor and windowsills were golden in the indirect sunlight. It was small, but private too, and filled with the quiet sound of the stream below. Julian had hooked up the heat to her room and put in the prettiest of the old grates we'd collected. Amelia, newly arrived from China, liked it too; it was just what she needed, and gradually she settled down.

One of the women I'd called for advice and information during the long wait had described to me the making of her new family. Her partner had arrived home with their baby all the way from Peru; the adoption had been a long and difficult process. They had been told they would adopt a tiny infant, but their daughter turned out to be ten months old and an early walker as well. This nice woman tried to explain how much had changed. Where there had been empty space, she said, now there was a little girl standing in the doorway; where there had been silence, now there was the sound of a child's footsteps. Where there had been no one just the day before, she said, now there was this small being, and their whole world was different.

We too had somehow managed to make room, and one

day there she was. Things fell into place around her. She'd lie in her little crib in the peaceful afternoon light, surrounded by teddy bears and rabbits and beautiful quilts sent by friends and neighbors and relatives. I moved a chest of drawers in for her and hung a print that a friend had given me many years before: a young Tibetan monk, a child really, sitting on the ground, playing a flute.

During the night we would tiptoe into the room to check on her; the dimmer allowed us to turn the light on just a bit. Sometimes she would be wide awake, lying on her back, holding her hands up and turning them slowly around, studying them from every angle, checking every finger. She was fine.

PHOTO ALBUM

IN THE FIRST few weeks, we took hundreds of pictures. I keep meaning to make a photo album for her, and I will, but they are still in a big box. I pick them out at random.

• A picture of Amelia in her brand-new stroller in the yard. The stroller has beautiful, big wheels, good for dirt roads. Amelia is so little! She is wearing a hat I bought her; it is much too big and hangs at a rakish angle, covering one ear. The bathtub is in the background, upside down on the grass. It still is. The planned bathroom has become a toolroom for now. Spot is standing by her. Spot died six months after, but Amelia still knows her by her picture.

• Amelia in my lap out by the garden. Spot is watching over her, and Lily is watching over me. Amelia is looking straight ahead; I am looking down. We are serious and calm; we look like we have already been through a lot together. We have. The garden is impressively overgrown. The lettuce has bolted into small trees, blossoms at the top bursting into hundreds and hundreds of tiny white flowers.

• Julian holding Amelia against his chest. She is wrapped in a big blanket with her hat still on. She looks safe. He looks happy and rather tired. They are sitting on the porch steps under the apple tree. The Buddha sits there too; he is a lawn ornament from Long Island.

• Julian has her in a baby backpack carrier; her head just barely peeks over the top. We have taken a walk up the hill. At the top is a dairy farm. Amelia and Julian are staring at a crowd of cows who are staring back.

• My sister Abby giving her a bottle. We're all sitting around the kitchen table. There is a little net for catching goldfish hung on the wall. I wonder, what is it doing there? Another yard sale item? All of Amelia is intent on her bottle. Everyone else is intent on Amelia.

• Julian and me sitting on the front porch, Amelia between us. There is a yellow ducky on the top step. The hummingbird feeder hangs behind us. We've probably forgotten to fill it lately. We are each holding one of Amelia's hands. Her hands are thin and delicate and perfect. She has thrown her hat on the ground, a challenge to the world. We face the camera squarely, triumphantly. We are all frowning a bit, but it's only the sun in our eyes.

HOME

IT SNOWED EARLY last winter, a sudden, wet snow that surprised the weathermen with its intensity and felled trees and power lines with its sheer weight. I had driven with Amelia and Lily to a distant town that day to do the laundry, always an excuse for an outing, and got caught in the storm on the way back just at nightfall. I hate driving in the snow. When I was younger, a lot younger, I didn't mind it so much; nothing had ever happened and I had no reason to think that anything ever would. But in the three years I've lived in Vermont I have skidded completely off the road three times. The first time was on a straight road covered with ice, going only fifteen miles an hour, which was fast enough to mash my bumper on one tree and crush my fender against another. The second time, I was going fifty miles an hour on a curvy road covered with ice, which was really, really dumb, and enough to rattle me forever, though I landed safely in a snowdrift. And the third time, I was going downhill in this early, wet snowstorm.

By the time I started down the long hill to my dirt road, it was pitch dark, and the snow almost blinding. There wasn't much accumulation, but a layer of heavy, slippery slush had spread over the pavement. I downshifted and tried to drive like a Vermonter should, or like I imagined a Vermonter should, realizing only later that few Vermonters were out driving that night at all.

I do know enough not to put on the brakes on a slippery road, but I probably did anyway. In my defense, it is very scary driving in a blinding snowstorm down a very steep hill, going faster and faster in second gear, with very, very little confidence in one's winter driving skills, with one's infant daughter in the backseat and one's lifelong pet in the front. I downshifted to first gear, probably put the brakes on, and immediately started to slide all over the road. Where I went off was luckily the uphill side of the road; we landed quite gently in the shallow ditch. Lily woke up with a grunt, and Amelia didn't even bother to take her bottle of juice out of her mouth.

I, however, was terrified. I thought that since I had gone off the road just there, maybe others would too. I saw us crushed by a truck. I saw terrible things, what might happen, what might have been. I bundled up Amelia in my arms and got us all out of the car as fast as I could.

The road we were on, or rather no longer on, is the main road down the hill, leading from the ridge at the top to the main valley at the bottom. The dirt road we live on turns off this road near the bottom almost at a hairpin angle, doubling back in a smaller valley below. Our house is a half mile or so down the dirt road. Rather than walk all the way down the slippery road to the dirt road just to double back on it, risking other reckless drivers skidding into us, I thought that it would be better to go overland. It was less than a mile, I figured, through a bunch of trees, across a sloping field, and finally down the hill through our overgrown apple orchard.

Lily was delighted, chasing flakes like a puppy, stopping to roll in the new, wet snow, scooping up mouthfuls, and snorting at the grass beneath. Amelia was clutching me, probably wondering why I was clutching her so hard, though I was trying not to act as panicky and upset and miserable as I felt.

It wasn't freezing cold, but my shoes were full of slush and my glasses were coated with snow. I couldn't see anything, it was slippery, Amelia was getting wet, it was as dark as it could possibly be, and my dog was paying no attention to me. Even though I had surely done more perilous and foolish things before in my life, I had never done anything quite like this. I was sure I would trip and fall with Amelia in my arms and we would lie there, broken-boned and covered with horrible snow. Lily would run for help but get lost. We would all die. I hadn't yet recovered from skidding off the road.

I tried to act like it was an adventure we just suddenly decided to take. A short detour, a slippery ride down a big slide. Amelia knew it was something more, though, turning in my arms to look into the darkness, turning back to watch my face, holding on tight when I almost stumbled. I tried to wrap her in my jacket and took off my snow-covered glasses so that we could see each other's eyes. Hers were wide and unafraid, taking it all in. By then we were out of sight of the main road; it was just the three of us, lost in that snowy night.

Only we weren't lost. Lily ran ahead to show us the way; she already knew. "What shall we do now? Which way shall we go? Now where are we, my best girl Amelia?" I was talking to my daughter, hoping to comfort her, even though she didn't seem to mind the strange journey we were on. We careened at a diagonal across a slippery patch of open field, and we were on our hillside. I stepped sideways down the steepest top part of the hill and turned past the rebuilt and unusable spring well. I sat right down in the snow, and we slid down another thirty feet. I shook off the slush, picked our way through the stumps of the hemlock trees that Julian and I had sawed down years before, and zigzagged a wet path down to level ground where Spot is buried. We almost tripped again, this time over the chicken wire fence around the vegetable garden, now half submerged in this new snow. At the next clump of old apple trees we caught up with Lily, and there it was. I'd left the lights on as usual, and through the snow and darkness I could see the distant glow of our oddly shaped house.

And then I heard Amelia's voice. She was answering me with her best new word. I heard her calling softly into the night. "Home," she said.

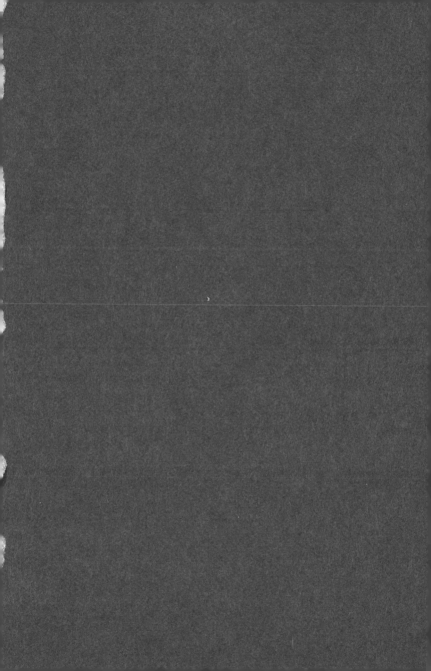